Stories From New India:
Policies, Hope And Change

Author
Dr.Somdutta Singh

INDIA • SINGAPORE • MALAYSIA

Notion Press Media Pvt Ltd

No. 50, Chettiyar Agaram Main Road,
Vanagaram, Chennai, Tamil Nadu – 600 095

First Published by Notion Press 2021
Copyright © Dr.Somdutta Singh 2021
All Rights Reserved.

ISBN 978-1-63873-591-5

Contents

Foreword

On May 23rd 2019, as I sipped my coffee on a bright Thursday morning stirring my brain to get dressed for work, I picked up the New York Times and the front page headline caught my attention straightway, "Narendra Modi, India's 'Watchman,' Captures Historic Election Victory." I then picked up the Wall Street Journal and there it was again, a headline glaring at my face, "India's Narendra Modi wins re-election with strong mandate."

That morning, Modi's win, landslide to say the least, after 600 million votes were cast over a period of 39 days did not really enthuse me. One of the biggest elections in history in one of the fastest growing nations of the world had just been single-handedly triumphed by one man, Narendra Modi and I found it particularly repetitive. This had happened earlier, 5 years to be precise. A naïve looking yet charismatic and polarising leader with exceptional linguistic efficacy, impregnable magnetism and grand gestures had led his party to a spectacular election victory and plundered the opposition.

The headlines that day were clearly not as unravelling to me as was the front-page headline on the Washington Post on May 26th, 2014 that had read, "Hindu nationalist Narendra Modi sworn in as India's Prime Minister." With the soaring cream-and-red sandstone dome of the president's house, the Rashtrapati Bhavan as a backdrop, there was a life-size portrait of Narendra Modi dressed in one of his trademark high-collared vests displayed across the front page. I starkly remember, in some way, the words 'Hindu nationalist' had caught my attention. Inexplicable questions lurked in my mind. Why was a newly appointed leader's religion, who had just shattered his opposition's decades long grip on the nation highlighted on a national daily headline in the United States? Throughout the article, why were there words like 'controversial leader', 'Hindu nation' and 'Hindutva ideology'?

That year, though I was away from the country, I was watching from the side lines. I was watching if the same moves would be made, I was watching if the same mandates that had won him the King's throne in 2014 would be implemented once again, I was watching if magnum opus Narendra Modi could weave his magic yet again. It finally dawned on me, that 2014 was no aberration, and that Indian politics has entered a new era of hegemony fuelled by Modi's extraordinary popularity. The poignant nationalism and Modi's personal magnetism were one aspect of the theatrics, the party's victory was unaided fuelled by a relentless, data-driven and highly disciplined style of campaigning. Somehow, after 2014, Modi's allure had started to wane, his mantra 'Achche din ayenge' or good days are coming was gradually becoming a millstone around his neck. Then wretched as it may sound, one bombing in Kashmir's disputed territory and Modi was back to transform the contest. Rather than dent Modi's strongman image, the carnage that left 40 paramilitaries deceased became the stage for his response, an airstrike deeper in neighbouring territory than Indian jets had ever struck.

Although I was born in India, I have lived in the United States for most of my adult life. I went to the States to complete my education wanting to back up my master's degree with a PhD. Then, after having established a row of successful businesses in India, I went back to the USA to test the waters for my various ventures and have since resided there.

India's melting pot of chaos, intoxication, beauty and illusions has always left me mesmerized. The explosion of colorful customs, an array of delightful traditions, a versatile terrain that changes every mile, India has always fascinated me. Everything, from the idyllic Himalayas to the backwaters in God's own country Kerala, from the life size boulders of

Hampi to a free-spirited Goa, India is mystifying yet crazy, exasperating yet delightful, squalid yet heartening and much more.

I have always had a keen interest in Indian politics. I have studied and monitored it closely. As an economist and businesswoman, I have followed India's developments and evolutions, upheavals and victories meticulously. While my lineages originally hail from Kolkata, it was the state of Gujarat that I had utmost interest in, the state that has been lauded for being the most investment-friendly state in India. Steering the wheels of the state was a man, the son of a grocer, a former *chaiwala* or tea seller who had come a long way in politics and taken the state to soaring heights. In a way, the name Gujarat was synonymous with advancement and triumph which was tantamount with one name – Narendra Damodardas Modi.

In 2013, Modi had completed 12 years of continuous rule as the Gujarat chief minister. Across the internet and throughout newspapers I reminisce having read how he had built his reputation in Gujarat as the state's Chief Minister on economic growth, building an efficient business administration and illustriously selling the state to the world. But, when foreigners tell stories about India, you only hear of constant power outages, bumpy roads and traffic and overwhelming crowds and poverty. This is only a fraction of the story. I had been intrigued to learn about this man, a new leader with the sole vision of building a new India, something he calls India 2.0.

Granted, Modi has been enigmatic, influential and enthralling, but, when a man comes to power to rule a nation marred with the baggage of corruption, unemployment and nepotism, the whole credit for such an annihilating victory cannot be given to the man and his charisma alone, right? The moniker for Modi's landslide victory had laid in the hands of India's 150 million 18-to 23-year-olds who had voted for the first time. In any nation, the youth are always the most aspirational; the most impatient, leading call for change. In India, the migration of the youth from rural to urban in search of employment has been accelerating colossally. This was a generation that had grown up after the 1991 liberalization of the Indian economy, as ushered in by India's then finance minister, Manmohan Singh. They were the only generation in the 67-year history of India to come of age in an atmosphere of unabated optimism because of continued growth. This national narrative received a deafening blow in 2011, with a recession that hit India after 20 years of growth. The more educated, young, urban Indian became disillusioned, dreams were shattered. Disillusionment with the ruling Congress was gradually creeping in and the anger, restlessness and frustration were growing. This disaffection had steered the young voter, the middle-class audience that was becoming more politically conscious towards the BJP —led by the charismatic and pro-business leader Narendra Modi. The consequence of the elections and Modi's glorious victory, in no small way made the voices of young India heard. He had established himself as a champion for industry and development. He is the son of a tea seller and his election was nothing short of a class revolt at the ballot box.

What I had liked about this man was that he had created an archetype that was above the party he represented, the BJP. He was an all-knowing father figure who was unwavering. He assured the people of India that when they voted for the Lotus sign, it was him they were voting for, not the party. He held himself responsible for the nation and not the party to do so. Narendra Modi was rewriting the rules of the game and redefining Indian politics. Brand Modi not only captured popular imagination but also trumped Brand BJP.

Now, as I write my story, although 1000s of miles away, I had kept a close watch on India, I wanted to witness first-hand how India has changed. Over the last three months, I have travelled extensively across the length and the breath of a nation, what is being called a New India — a country that is hopeful, proud and prosperous. Administered by a new government with a fresh outlook to bring about transformation, to bring about a revolution, I wanted to see how the visionary headlines about policies that have been introduced by Modi, have they been only on paper or have they been implemented already? I wanted to observe the precise influence the new government has been able to create through its policies, innovations and ideologies. How was the country doing in which for almost three decades, a leader was not as important as the collective called the party and abstracts like ideologies?

I wanted to witness after returning Modi back to power with such a thumping mandate, was India on its course to becoming a $5 trillion economy witnessing inclusive development and spurring growth? As India's innings begin with a new set of ministers, how is the nation defining its place in the world? While India needs the West for its growth spurt, the West needs India for its booming markets and gigantic human resource pools. How is India looking to foster its association with China and Japan? Is the observable camaraderie between leaders enough to adjust and move quickly in a rapidly changing world milieu?

Through the course of my journey, I met people from diverse backgrounds. Though culturally rich in every context, people in India hail from different circumstances, educational backgrounds, ideologies and narrate an assortment of stories. Stories that reflect how India had evolved and metamorphosed from 1947 until today. Stories that illustrate and elucidate the tangible impact a government can have on its people. Stories that will touch your heart and open your minds towards a nation that is beloved, sacred and reveals a cultural chasm at every corner that you turn at.

As I went from state to state in my India, the product of the fluid forces of great migrations and interactions that shaped this country, I came across tales – untold, dazzling and exotic. These tales needed to be told. The world needed to know these stories as they unraveled in front of my eyes.

✳ ✳ ✳

J.A. Choudhary – The origin of these tales lay in a conversation Som and I had ages ago. From the moment I have known Som, she was totally focused, her competitiveness and no-nonsense attitude was evident in everything she did and has been doing since. Writing is hard, even for seasoned writers, but for Dr. Som, words flow naturally to her, which is very evident in the tales she has narrated in this book. They are passionate, authentic and defined.

* * *

Ana Roy – This book captures the very essence of living and shows it is more than just a fable, a parable or a pipe dream. It›s real; the stories are true and show how the world truly works. Her stories touch lives, expanding the circle of being open to receiving as well as giving. This book serves as a repository of valuable information under a novel administration and powerful leader.

* * *

Anuj Jain – We have witnessed a paradigm shift in India's politics. With his clean reputation, proven track record as chief minister and formidable leadership qualities on display, Narendra Modi seemed the right fit for the prime minister's job, and just the man to turn the country around. While Prime Minister Modi's first term raised troubling questions, he has ensured that India has evolved dramatically in the socio-political and economic milieu. This book, through lovely tales of hope and affection offers a perspective that helps explain India's stand in a global forum. The stories are argumentative and thought-provoking. This book is a must-read.

– 1 –

Voicing My Memories: The Day I Was Born In India

I am inside my mother's womb, the utero, enclosed within a weightless, fluid-filled environment, an environment that keeps me safe, secure and sheltered from external toxins. I can comprehend every move my mother makes. Each time she caresses her stomach, I dance within her. Each time she sings to me, I recognize which song it is. It gets miserable in here when she's depressed, I get ecstatic when she's cheerful. Though I can't see a thing in here, a new lease of life charges through the tiniest fibre of my being and I know the world that awaits me is beautiful, full of light and opportunities, a melting pot of cultures.

If you are wondering vis-à-vis what is driving me to be so optimistic, I have my reasons and they are persuasive, you'll see. When I was no less than the size of a peanut, my mother's eyes narrated a harrowing tale – they were dull, helpless and pale as she waited her turn to be examined by the doctors at a nongovernmental organization in Calcutta that worked with the underprivileged. At times, during check-ups, my mother even had to share a bed with another mother. I wince when I envision the horror she had to endure. She could neither afford a doctor nor buy medicines. She trudged miles in the wee hours of cold mornings to attain free medical treatment.

My mother was severely under-nourished and anemic. This was adversely affecting her health and in turn mine. When poor nutrition starts in utero, it inevitably extends throughout the life cycle since the changes are largely irreversible. My mother worked as a domestic help, washing dishes, scrubbing dirty laundry, but when I was there within her, she lost her job. My father could barely make ends meet with the meagre amount he earned pulling rickshaw carts around town.

It is no wonder that in India, every 8 minutes, a mother dies during childbirth and pregnancy related complications. Regrettably, these demises are largely avertible, nonetheless, owing to poor access to health services and lack of proper pregnancy care, they aren't. The poor state of maternal health in India has long been on the global radar in the world's fastest-growing economy.

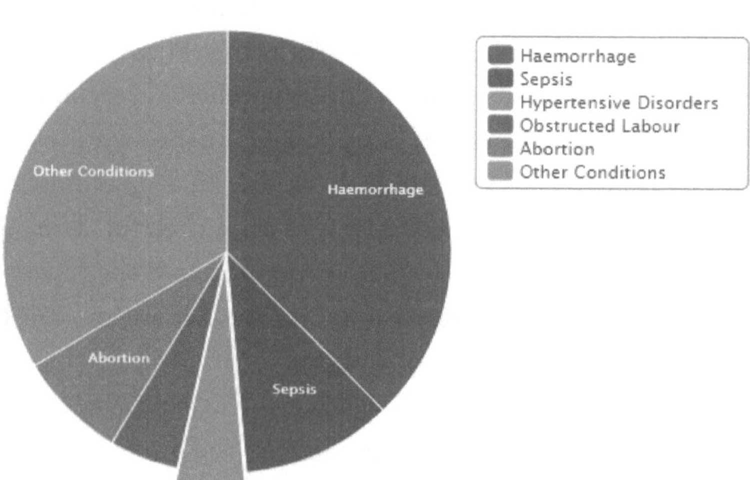

Childbirth, though a cheerful event for the affluent, brings with it myriad fears and traumas for the deprived. My mother, at the time required attention, respect and gentle guidance. When women are humiliated, abused and denied basic comforts, care and a healthy birthing environment, it is a matter of grave concern and disgrace for all of humankind, don't you think? Having a baby in a remote village of Calcutta, meant being pregnant with anxiety and a sense of helplessness. Without access to health infrastructure and trained medical personnel to monitor pregnancies and provisions for emergency care, it was a life-threatening situation for my mother and me. While India's public health system has been grappling with a dearth of health facilities, shortage of human resources is one of the biggest impediments to the functioning of existing public health facilities. The absence of health centers in close proximity also meant that pregnant women, like my mother had to travel long distances to avail basic medical services.

However, within the next few months, a positive transformation in the atmosphere was tangible. Rigorous efforts are being made by administering bodies to improve maternal health by encouraging institutional deliveries that will in turn reduce the global burden of preventable maternal, neonatal and child deaths. Implementing policies and programs that benefit women and most importantly, save their lives have yielded enormous results across the nation. In 2000, when countries across the world had joined hands to commit towards achieving Millennium Development Goals by 2015, India's share of maternal deaths was alarmingly nearly a quarter of the global burden. Astoundingly, maternal mortality rate has drastically plummeted by 22% over the last few years, on account of our rapid developmental progress. In a nation where the world's 1/5th babies are born, this means fewer pregnant women are dying during childbirth or from pregnancy-related complications, bringing India's share of global maternal death burden to near 10% for the first time ever.

India's progress has been much higher and rapid than the global average, with India registering a 77% decline in MMR from 1990 to 2015 as compared to 44% worldwide. If we accomplish objectives at this rate, India will achieve its Sustainable Development Goals target of 70 MMR by 2022, eight years ahead of the scheduled deadline. This is not just an indicator of advanced maternal health but also a pronouncement of India's socioeconomic development and health. There has been an increase of 39% and 14.6% in the number of community health centres (CHCs) and primary health centres (PHCs) respectively in just the last few months. There has also been an addition of 73,268 female health workers at sub-centres and 4,516 doctors at PHCs. Multi-skilling of doctors and scaling up of emergency transport has also been fast-tracked speedily. Accredited Social Health Activists (ASHAs) have played a critical role in awareness-building and bringing pregnant women to healthcare institutions. These recent results that illustrate the decline in maternal mortality should be taken only as an opportunity to step up the pace of decline with stronger and sustained government commitment, a favorable policy environment and well-targeted resources.

All the more so, Empowered Action Group (EAG) states in India which include Bihar, Chhattisgarh, Jharkhand, Madhya Pradesh, Orissa, Rajasthan, Uttaranchal and Uttar Pradesh that lag in health indicators, demographic transition and have the highest infant mortality rates in the country have revealed a significant 23.6% decline. These beyond belief variations in neonatal mortality suggest that universal coverage of all pregnant women with full antenatal care, providing assistance at delivery and postnatal care including emergency care are being rapidly intensified. Health interventions that focus on curtailing the high risk of neonatal deaths arising from the mothers' immature age at childbirth, low birth weight of children and higher order births with short birth intervals are also been monitored and accelerated.

Still inside my mother's womb, when I was finally big enough to sense the world around me, I could fathom that my mother was being offered appropriate care in the new center she was visiting. At the new centre my mother went to, Anganwadis which is roughly translated as 'courtyard shelters', my mother was being counselled and educated about child delivery, optimal breastfeeding, child growth monitoring, immunizations and proper newborn care by accredited social health activists. Likewise, when my mother had any queries on the subject of the unknown territory she was steeping into, all she had to do was call a toll-free helpline that has been launched to address queries associated with nutrition and malnutrition, a focus area that necessitates foremost responsiveness.

At a far distance, I often also overhear my mother listening to an exchange of ideas that is spreading awareness about Poshan Abhiyan, an operation that aims to bridge the nutrition gap and bring down stunting among children in the age group 0-6 years from 38.4% to 25% by 2022. Research has shown that by ensuring supplementary nutrition for children in the 0-3 years' age bracket, the number of graduates in India can proliferate by an enormous 3.17 million – from the current 7.5% of India's 73.8 million 20-24-year-olds to 11.8%. This new generation of healthier and brighter progenies will consecutively deliver momentous economic gains from higher wages. This will be a substantial economic achievement for a nation with one in four of the world's 156 million stunted under-five-year-olds.

In a concerted effort to eradicate malnutrition, Poshan Abhiyan is first of its kind initiative launched to tackle malnutrition through multimodal interventions. It seeks to reduce malnutrition through convergence, use of technology & a targeted approach and ensure India is malnutrition free by 2022 and thereby safeguard holistic development and adequate nutrition for pregnant women, mothers and children. Poshan Abhiyaan, under the aegis of the Ministry of Women and Child Development is creating a robust convergence synergy by mapping various schemes across India that are contributing towards addressing malnutrition, incentivizing Anganwadi healthcare workers for employing IT based tools and setting-up Nutrition Resource Centres that encourage our communities to play a part in the numerous activities that place prominence on nutrition.

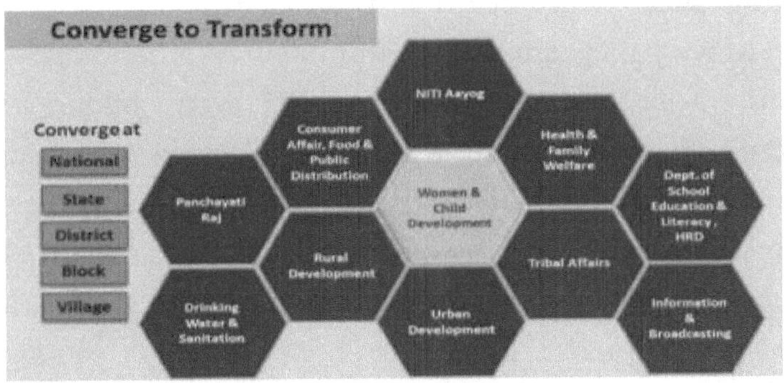

There's also proof that children who attained extra nutrition through government-run programmes from the time they were in their mothers' wombs until age 3 were 11% more likely to acquire a graduate degree than those who received them between ages 3 and 6. Adequate nutrition during what is called the 1,000-day-window-of-opportunity – the time between pregnancy and a child's 2nd birthday is identified to defend children against stunting and cognitive deficiencies. Scientists have monitored the lives of children and mothers at *Anganwadis* and have discovered positive health impacts that persist till adolescence.

Correspondingly, under the Pradhan Mantri Matru Vandana Yojana (PMMVY) and Janani Suraksha Yojana, Maternity Benefit Programmes for pregnant and lactating mothers, my mother received a cash transfer of Rs 6000, something of utmost importance in the unorganized sector considering they make up 90% of the India's female workforce. The financial support and maternity benefits my mother received compensated for the wage loss while also ensuring she was getting the requisite nutrition, rest and most importantly, peace of mind. My mother did not have the fear to let go of her work, which often compels women in the informal sector to work through pregnancy and immediately thereafter, to the detriment of their and their babies' health.

With the purpose of ensuring affordable and quality healthcare, 1084 essential medicines, including lifesaving drugs have been brought under the price control regime. Affording medicine for my parents is no more a luxury.

Bringing about change in a country as large and diverse as India is no small feat. Moving pregnant women from houses to hospitals for delivery and ensuring skilled birth attendants deliver every child is imperative. Just a decade ago, a little more than half of all births were happening at home, but the introduction of cash transfers for institutional deliveries has led to more than 8 out of 10 women delivering at a health centre and our resilient administration is ensuring that such efforts are backed up by quality and respectful care. Sensitive to these challenges, our government recently also launched the LaQshya initiative for labour-room quality of care improvement. Advancing on the path chosen will require a strong focus on quality as envisioned.

Another challenge that India encounters is to provide skilled birth attendance and a safe pair of hands for the 50 lakh pregnant women still delivering at home. Several training packages such as Life Saving Anaesthesia

Skills, Comprehensive and Basic Emergency Obstetric Care, Daksh and Dakshata trainings for quality intrapartum care have been implemented. The Janani Shishu Suraksha Karyakram (JSSK) which provides free transport and care to pregnant women during childbirth are initiatives to encourage access to institutional delivery to women from the poorest quintile households. Also, on the 9th of every month, my mother attains assured, comprehensive and quality antenatal care, free of cost under the Pradhan Mantri Surakshit Matritva Abhiyan for ensuring good health of mother and child. So far, more than 1.3 crore antenatal check-ups have been conducted at over 13,078 health facilities. Further, more than 80.63 lakh pregnant women have been immunized and during screening, more than 6.5 lakh high risk pregnancies have been identified.

The day finally came. One winter night, I couldn't stay in any longer. I was roaring to come out. An old haggard woman was summoned home. Everyone was referring to her as 'dai ma'. My father's joys knew no bounds; my mother's screams were ear-piercing. I knew she was in pain, but what could I do? My grandfather was ecstatic; he would soon get his rightful 'heir'. I used to see how often the highly respected dowagers of my neighbourhood would spare a few moments to survey the shape of my mother's pregnant belly and gleefully pass the verdict, "Mone hoche, chele hobey!" (Looks like you're going to have a boy). My mother politely brushed aside the talks with a soft smile. I knew, my father and mother were far more concerned about my health than my gender.

Fittingly, my mother did prove predictions right and I was born. Just after delivering me, her first-born, my mother screamed, "I actually did it! He is finally here!" That was the moment I realised, the valour, strength and power this woman possesses is unimaginable. The air of happiness was palpable amongst the elderly; my parents were equally rejoicing.

Within minutes, my father rushed me to the nearest Anganwadi centre which I was told was going to be my home for the next few days. First time parents, my mother and father, who live a good one hour away from the nearest Anganwadi centre were assured that their day-old baby would be in good hands and taken care of aptly. At the centre, trained health personnel quickly took my weight and other assessments were done in no time. My parents were given advice on nutrition and immunizations, an intervention that has drastically altered the lives of people in my village. There are mothers who have had healthy pregnancies, normal deliveries and beaming, healthy babies. Although many of the mothers are unlettered, they now know more about parenting and how to keep their children healthy and happy than before. On account of initiatives such as these and the workforces at the helm, numerous life-threatening cases have been detected early and lives have been salvaged.

The state I am born in, West Bengal, just a few years back was witness to abysmal conditions of neonatal care. Child mortality rate was at an all-time high with thousands perishing before they could even crawl. Today, a shining beacon of hope, the state is propelling up the development index.

At the Anganwadi center, I cannot fail to notice the fact that this army of women, 28 lakh across India, is working relentlessly on the frontlines to provide supplementary nutrition, immunisation, referral services, health check-ups, pre-school non-formal education and health and nutrition education to 10 crore beneficiaries at 14 lakh anganwadi centres across the country. They are playing a crucial role in helping India achieve its health and nutrition goals. For the sake of the beneficiaries, like my mother and I, of the various government programs these women work for, they definitely deserve greater attention. We have to realize that, only by providing adequate services to them will our government and society move towards reducing, recognizing and redistributing the burden of unpaid care work that women in India disproportionately bear? Elimination of hunger, reducing maternal and child mortality and recognizing unpaid care work are part of the United Nations' Sustainable Development Goals, objectives that India has also endorsed.

Without schooling, millions of children are pushed into child labour and condemned to a life of social exclusion, low earnings and exploitation. Some of them even work for dangerously long hours as domestic helps or are forced into begging and prostitution or wind-up becoming rag-pickers. When they grow up, they swell the ranks of unskilled labor at the lowest rung of our society and are denied equal opportunities and choices. For the reason that the first 6 years of a child's life are most vulnerable for rapid human development, ICDS or Integrated Child Development Services play an intervening role of great consequences. They provide young children with an integrated package of services such as supplementary nutrition, healthcare and pre-school education which helps lay the foundation for a child's proper psychological, physical, aesthetic and social development.

Over the years, poor infrastructure and low wages have taken a toll on workers' motivation levels which has at times encouraged corruption. Pilferage of food meant for distribution to malnourished children is common. The Prime Minister's Office has propositioned bar code technology to check this leakage. Acting quickly on this, the women and child development ministry has introduced smartphones for all workers to usher in real-time monitoring of the *anganwadi* services. With the ability to identify and monitor the progress of every malnourished child, improvement in health outcomes will be perceptible. Pilferage will be examined by requiring workers to scan a barcode on the packet of take-home ration, prior to distribution and add that information to the beneficiary profile maintained on a database accessible by supervisors.

Childhood years are foundational in deciding the health of individuals. Our government's Mission Indradhanush aims to cover all the children who are either unvaccinated or are partially vaccinated against seven vaccine preventable diseases which include diphtheria, whooping cough, tetanus, polio, tuberculosis, measles and hepatitis B. Thus far, the mission has accomplished four phases covering 528 districts wherein 82 lakh pregnant women have been immunized and 3.2 crore children vaccinated. It was only in November 2015 that Inactivated Polio Vaccine (IPV), which is much more effective than oral vaccine was introduced. Roughly 4 crore doses have already been administered to children. Rotavirus Vaccine that was launched in March 2016 has already witnessed nearly 1.5 crore dose administration.

Also, in my village, within the next 2 years, under the Atal Mission for Rejuvenation and Urban Transformation (AMRUT) scheme, we will have access to a tap with assured supply of water and a sewerage connection and other amenities that will radically improve the quality of life for all. My mother will not have to travel miles to fetch water from the river and we will no longer be susceptible to diseases, illnesses that have taken the lives of numerous in my hamlet. Alongside this, my parents' dreams of possessing a house may soon materialize with our Prime Minister approving more houses to be built under the Pradhan Mantri Awas Yojana that will not just alleviate poverty in India, but also give a much required boost to our real-estate market thus escalating our economy.

They say, good is not good if better is possible. It's about time we abandoned the 'chalta hai' attitude and contemplate on the 'badal sakta hai' mindset! With the strong leadership at the center, intense commitments from states and the tireless efforts of millions of health workers, India will become a beacon of hope, will give the world a new headline.

I Broke Free From The Chains Of Patriarchy: The Day I Joined School

I am Titli, I am 4 and I live in Bihar. Bihar, the state where women were once looked upon as second-class citizens, the state where despite having fought and won several battles challenging deep-rooted prejudice and stereotypes, women have consistently remained at the bottom of statistics sweepstakes, the state that had been infamous for tales of rape, murder, domestic violence and dowry deaths so harrowing, they send shivers down one's spine, the state that had been written off by India.

The situation was no different for my mother and her antecedents. She had grown up in a traditional household where authority was absolute. Although my family has asserted, they are 'modern' in their outlook, women in the house were bound to listen to orders and follow them blindly. Once married, their oppression was normalized as 'obligations' she must fulfill towards her husband and his family. Regrettably, they were conditioned to believe that marriage legitimizes male authority. They counted themselves fortunate to not have been killed while in their mother's womb or soon after they were born. Every day was a struggle against handicaps and social evils in a male-dominated society. They were powerless and frightened.

After I was born, things changed one way or another. I was born a girl in a land where poverty, low social development and patriarchal institutions ruled. Investments on girls were not just limited, but, with Bihar having the lowest female literacy rate and the highest female infanticide rate in the country, women were considered inferior to their male counterparts and families have long since discouraged girls from taking up studies.

My mother chose to fight for me. In the face of adversity, against the voices of the male members of my family, my mother decided to become an agent of change, champion my rights and in turn bring about a transformative impact that was never even mulled over before. When I ask her, what gave her the courage to rebel, here's what she says dramatically. "When Malala Yousafzai was just 15, she was shot in the head by the Taliban in Pakistan. You know why? All she wanted to do was study, get an education. I did not get the opportunity because my mother did not have the courage or in the midst of all hardships and constantly demanding household chores, she did not have time to muster the courage. I will not let that happen to you. If Malala could have taken a bullet, so could I. I wanted to lead a pioneering change in attitudes that men in our societies have for women, an attitude that your grandparents and father had towards you when you were born."

That was probably the moment that must have made the 'power-bearers' of my family, the men shudder. My mother's plea was simple, to send me to school along with the sons of the house. Figures from UNICEF in 2016 showed that about 32 million girls of primary school age and 29 million of lower secondary school age worldwide are not getting an education. Half a billion women still cannot read and 62 million girls around the world are not in primary or secondary school. These statistics are incriminatory and depressing, aren't they?

I could never understand why I wasn't given a bag filled with colourful books, bid adieu by dadu dadi and sent to the place my bhaiyas went to? I could never understand why bhaiyas were stopped each time they wanted to play ghar-ghar with me? I could never understand why chachi always skipped the chapter that narrated the tale of the valiant warrior princess, swords blazing atop a mighty horse? I would enviously look at my bhaiyas' crisp yellow and green uniforms and new books. They even had new bicycles to go to school on!

Each day, why are millions of children, read girls like me fighting to get basic education? In a country that has a national literacy rate of 74.04% with Bihar at 63.82%, is attaining a right to education so tough, merely because I am a girl? When Malala was shot, millions globally expressed their solidarity with her by doing the obligatory status update or tweet: "We are all Malala". But, for the rest, she was just someone else's child and will remain so forever. She is a child whose name can be invoked to start another military operation, a child whose name can be used to prove the blindingly obvious – that parents, whatever their religion or culture, would like their children to be at school – if they can afford it. Agreed! But, what is conveniently ignored in this debate is that every 10th child in the world who doesn't go to school is a girl.

Why is an educated female population seen as more threatening than armies equipped with dreadful drones? Every girl who crams for a high-school exam, every woman who runs a hospital and every illiterate mother who fights for her daughter to get a better education than herself, is still seen as a mortal threat to our 'educated' society? By abdicating our responsibilities to educate the girl child, to protect those who manage to go to school and those who teach them, aren't we making it that much easier for groups like Taliban's mission to succeed?

I have overheard my dadu telling my father how abhiyans or policies like Samagra Shiksha are ensuring universal access to education and treating education holistically without segmentation. Prepared with the broader goal of improving school effectiveness measured in terms of equal opportunities for schooling and equitable learning outcomes, such schemes are guaranteed to strengthen capacities by improving quality of education with 2 T's – Teachers and Technology and encourage more parents to send their children, especially the girl child to schools. If they have to fulfil their potential, girls need to have equal opportunities and getting an education is the first stepping stone.

If current trends continue, 8 million boys around the world will never go to school. Shocking isn't it? Of course it is. But, here's something more staggeringly outrageous. Twice as many girls will never set foot inside a classroom and learn to read and write, unless of course, things change dramatically.

March 8 is International Women's Day and in 2017, the theme was "Planet 50-50 by 2030". That means ensuring equality in education, economic opportunities and human rights as laid out in the 15-year Sustainable Development Goals agreed by world leaders. We talk about achieving soaring Sustainable Development Goals, but I ask you, without overcoming the discrimination and poverty that stunt the lives of girls and women from one generation to the next, how are you planning to achieve this?

When the day for me to go to school finally came, I asked Ma, "If I am prevented from going, the place must be bad, but then why do bhaiyas go?" My mother beamingly said, "As a girl in India, life doesn't give you choices. You either stand up and create them, or you stay put and give in. I will swim against the current to ensure you get an education that will guarantee the independence I never got." That moment, I knew, I had to fight my way to the top, not for myself, not for the world, but for the woman sitting in front of me with her head buried under the ghunghat.

She added, "Today, organizations and the government is working at all levels, from grassroots to global leaders, to put equity and inclusion at the heart of every policy so that all girls, whatever their circumstances, go to school, stay in school and become empowered citizens." Something in me beamed. Under our Right to Education (RTE) Act, passed in 2009, a free and compulsory education is guaranteed for all children aged between 6 and 14 and recent figures for primary school enrolment do stand out at an impressive number – 98% as of 2015. Our leaders at the helm are leading the way, not only in making women-centric policies a focal point of governance but also in ensuring better representation in positions of power. There is a strong emphasis on mindset change through training, sensitization, awareness raising and community mobilization on the ground.

What India needs today is a transformational shift in the way we, our society looks at the girl child. We need to glorify the Sarpanch from Bibipur in Haryana who started a 'Selfie with Daughter' initiative. Within no time, the inventiveness harvested massive fanfare, not just in India, but internationally. People from across India and the world shared their selfies with their daughters, a proud occasion for the nation.

In India, the country that is marred with female feticide, structures like Beti Bachao- Beti Padao are finally addressing gender imbalance and discrimination against the girl child. Multi-sectoral District Action Plans need to be operationalized across states and capacity-building programmes and trainings need to be imparted to trainers to further strengthen capacities of district level officials and frontline workers. I recall, a few years back, a boy named Prince had fallen into a tube well in a remote village of Kurukshetra district of Haryana. Instantly, it garnered national attention with millions glued to their television sets to follow his rescue updates. Millions prayed for him. I ask you, why don't we show the same concern for the lakhs, if not millions who are killed in the womb?

Have you ever thought that if the present gender imbalance endured, what the repercussion would be like? For every 1,000 boys, 1,000 girls should be born. Let's take examples of Mahendergarh and Jhajjar districts where there are merely about 775 girls for 1,000 boys deserting 225 boys to be left unmarried. In Haryana, the sex ratio in the districts ranges between 875 and 837 which means for every 1,000 boys about 125 to 150 girls are being killed. If there were no selective abortions, female infanticide, or deliberate neglect, women would outnumber men there. India is the land of the missing millions – more than 63 million women are missing across India and more than 21 million girls are unwanted by their families. Crimes against women are the highest in the country, and more than a third of them are perpetrated by husbands and other male relatives.

If daughters are not born or are not allowed to be born, where will you get your bahus from? I am sure you want an educated daughter-in-law for your son, but, did you think once about educating your mother or sister? Educating our daughters is our responsibility.

Once I started going to school, my mother made a promise, a pledge more to herself than me that she will open an account in my name under the Sukanya Samriddhi Scheme that will allow her to save how much ever she can amass for my education. With programs such as these, our government is effortlessly trying to encourage financial inclusion and increase domestic savings that has seen a nose-dive in prior years. Focusing on the twin challenges of a quality and an affordable education is the only way to break a vicious cycle that has rendered women powerless, generation after generation. We need to smash the patriarchy that has deprived women of agency, women who are killed for not having a large enough dowry; who commit suicide more than any other female demographic.

I have always been obsessed with one perplexing question: What keeps India from excelling? Why, for instance, do Indian Americans have the highest average household income of all ethnic groups in the US, yet in India, one in four citizens still live in abject poverty?

Here's my theory. My homeland, India has been crippled by its total subjugation of women. From not receiving their fair share of inheritance to being forced to marry older men as a payback for loans, women are systematically deprived of their human rights – and the country of half its potential.

We need to get one thing straight. Women's empowerment cannot be complete without the education of girls. Now, educating the girl child not just refers to every aspect of schooling that aims at developing their skill and knowledge base, it equally includes technical training, financial literacy and vocational edification in order to make them self-governing. When the girl child is educated, she has the ability to bring about changes in the nation so powerful that economies can stir. Primary education is a key right. When a girl is protected through her rights, the society is assured of its sustainability. Education offers women a path to economic independence and help them gain social power.

We have a strong governance at the helm with a powerful vision. All it needs is kindness, fierceness and pragmatism. Female literacy is one of the most powerful levers to improve a society's health and economic well-being. Ensuring that the girl child is educated sets off a virtuous chain reaction – improved literacy leading to delayed age of marriage, fewer and healthier children and corresponding reduction in poverty.

More than anything today, our mantra should be, 'Beta Beti, Ek Samaan'. We should celebrate the birth of the girl child and be equally proud of our daughters. Empowerment of women is an important precondition for the development of not just a nation's economy but humanity at large. It is most definitely a matter of pride that women are increasingly playing bigger roles in the development of the nation, right from cities and villages up to the seats of power.

Today I am in Standard V and am an embodiment of potential. In a remote town of Bihar where most homes have no toilets, and barely any electricity, I stand out even when I walk the streets. I have the valor to not lower my eyes when I navigate the tiny alleys threaded between our homes where street urchins loom large. Thanks to the education I received, I exude the strength of someone who has been taught her worth. I want to become a corporate lawyer and move to California someday to practice. With each passing day as I tread the 4 kilometer journey between my home and school, that dream gets closer. Whether I go to work in the US – or, more likely to Kolkata or Delhi – I will be the first person from my community to do so. There is no doubt in my mind – I am destined for great things – not despite being a girl, but because I am one.

It Took My Country 157 Years to Acknowledge Who I Truly Am

I was born Nishant in a small hamlet in Kerala, about two hours from the state capital Trivandrum. At first I was reticent and withdrawn, I did not fathom why? I was born a boy, but I knew something wasn't right. The jingling of ghungroos when my sister danced in the large courtyard at the back and the beats of music her guru played enthralled me. They sent ripples of pleasure through my body. As a little boy, I loved giving grand performances in front of my neighbors and relatives. It was taken in a lighter vein.

Surprisingly, at that time, no one was anxious to know what made me do what I was doing or to identify what my thoughts were. That's probably because they had no knowledge that a third gender existed or plainly because being one was a 'curse', an abomination so horrifying, it was not even spoken of. Even as a child, this raised questions in my mind. By self-expressing myself, was I bringing about an imbalance in the society I lived in? My thoughts were ambiguous; my judgements were abstruse.

The first time I realized I was in a wrong body was perhaps during my 5th standard at school. I felt different, but was not able to put my finger on exactly what that meant. I was born a boy, but I did not feel like one. I struggled to make friends and experienced both anxiety and despair. My self-confidence was unprecedentedly low. Even though I had a male body, my thinking, my habits were feminine. I liked talking to girls, I loathed boys. My internal gender identity somehow did not match the sex I had been assigned at birth. A lot of people, especially the aunts and uncles of my neighborhood thought that we wake up one day and decide to become a transgender. I want you to know that it's not a choice I made calculatedly. Nothing has happened in my life that 'made' me a Trans. I was born one.

But, I did not have the courage to discuss this with anyone. It was forbidden. I was surrounded by insecurities. I was confused with what was happening to me and my body.

I was constantly mocked and bullied by my classmates. During my teen years, my traditional father and uncles constantly exclaimed, "Act like a man, you are going to bring shame to our family with your bizarre shenanigans!" Bizarre? Really? I was simply being myself. I withdrew into my shell. I was always a bright student, only attaining the top ranks in school, until the teasing and taunting left me traumatized. My behavior was so feminine that no matter who looked at me, mocked me, ridiculed me and imitated me. Within the safe confines of my home, I loved dressing up in my mother's sarees and applying make-up. I vividly remember the day my father caught me red-handed in my mother's stunning red kanjeevaram, an heirloom that had been in my family for generations, and got so furious that he charred it to ashes. Even today, when I reminisce that day, shivers run down my spine.

One fine day, in one of my Biology lessons, my teacher introduced us to genetic disorders, chromosomes and reproductive organs. I studied for hours on the internet and read about transgenders. Suddenly, everything made sense, everything sounded normal, and everything fell into place. There was one thing I distinctly understood that day – nature was not made of just two colors – black and white. It has myriad, infinite shades of gray. That day I came to terms with the fact – I was a woman trapped in a man's body.

I may have acknowledged the woman within me, my family never did. One day, when I mustered courage and finally revealed my true self, my parents were unnerved. More than assenting to the fact that their beloved son was coming to terms with his sexual identity, they were livid that I could even envisage something so atrocious. For them, it was an amusing story, a story that needed to be forgotten.

But, when I put my foot down asserting, I will no more be the object of ridicule, it took my father less than a few seconds to renounce me, to chuck me out of my home, the shelter I thought was the only place on Earth I was safe in. In a matter of minutes, I was rendered homeless, ostracized by society. Not even a few meters away from home, a gully where I used to play as a child, I was sexually assaulted by the chettans of my neighborhood, some of them, brothers of my friends. Our cultural ideals voice that men are capable of perpetrating violence; women are subject to this violence. The third sex on the other hand, a transgender sans no legal recognition, an unmoved society and an emotionally impassive family was the easiest target. In accordance with latest census, there are more than 2 million transgender people in India and 95% of them are leading a life that is not worth living.

Broken yet determined, I moved cities. The year was 2009. From Kerala, I moved to maximum city Mumbai. After several years, though battered by the storm that almost smothered my life, I was determined to find a ray of sunshine. In the fast-paced city that Mumbai was illustrious for, an old woman did shelter me. She was a transgender, a human being who had long lost hopes to get acknowledged in India. "Gain knowledge my child. Knowledge will enlighten your path." The old lady had said to me as she wiped my misty eyes and wrapped her arms tightly around me. "It is never too late." Resolute, I enrolled at a vocational training institute to study digital marketing, a domain I knew was flourishing, a domain where there was a huge gap between available jobs and acquiring accomplished digital marketers to fill them. But, who'll give me a job? I was a transgender. The year was 2012.

In India, the transgender community had been among the most marginalized with access to education and subsequently jobs mostly nonexistent. Gay sex was a criminal offence under Section 377 and some cardinal questions always remained. Whether the Colonial-era draconian law met the test of constitutionality? Was it in tune with the fundamental rights gifted to every citizen by the Constitution? Did its presence hinder individuals from enjoying their human rights that they are entitled to by the virtue of them being humans? There was a lot being written about the array of arguments in favour of and against the rights of the LGBTQ community. Discussions on Section 377 popped up terms like "gay sex", "same-sex" and "gay rights". This wasn't merely limited to casual conversations over chai; they made headlines in newspapers, websites, blogs, TV debates, Facebook posts and WhatsApp messages.

Finally, in 2014, the Supreme Court passed a landmark judgement, paving the way for enshrining the rights of transgenders in law. Trans individuals like me had the right to self-identification of their sexual orientation as the third gender and that fundamental rights granted by India's Constitution were made equally applicable to us. Thanks to our powerful leaders who have fought relentless battles with the Supreme Court questioning the "political" and "practical" ramifications of the judgment, rights long denied to us looked just a hand away. With a fresh face at the helm of the governance, empowered by its decidedly fresh outlook, India is finally drifting away from its apologizing attitude, its subservience to the West and an inward looking socialism. India has witnessed a paradigm shift in the way its policies have been governed, its people aspects have been evaluated and considered and in the way governance has been administered.

In India, opposition to moves that have been fighting to overturn such primeval laws have rested predominately on religious and moral objections and by the middle and lower classes who are drenched in prejudice. I have studied our scriptures and Vedas meticulously. Fascinatingly, India was once at ease with depictions of same-sex love and gender fluidity and Hinduism has traditionally maintained a very flexible, non-prescriptive view of sexuality. Gods transformed into goddesses and men bore children. Centuries-old Hindu temples depict erotic encounters between members of the same sex. Rekhti, a genre of poetry that flourished in India from the late 1700s, describes erotic encounters between women. In certain other cultures, transgender people have been given special status and praised for being loyal.

But the culture of tolerance changed drastically under the British colonization at the height of the Victorian era. When the English arrived, the acceptance of homosexuality eroded. With time, hardline religious groups have taken a more conservative approach. If India has to operate as part of the global economy, it's not just GDP numbers that will make it a part – it's these inclusive values that will.

Finally, in 2018, Section 377, one of the most hidebound relics of India's colonial past was buried. After 157 years, one of the most glaring vestiges of India's colonial past was let go. We are the world's largest democracy and in an egalitarian society like ours, the power vests in our hands, the citizens, we hand-pick our governments after all, don't we? But, sadly, Section 377 was struck down by 5 people sitting in a courtroom and not by the legislation, the law governing body for India's citizens.

Disgust and contempt were central themes of section 377 since its inception. In 1830 Thomas Macaulay, the main drafter of the code, called homosexual sex "odious" and "revolting". In 1934, a judge in Sindh, now Pakistan described a man who had consensual sex with another man as "a despicable specimen of humanity". In 2003, the government of India said that decriminalizing homosexuality would "open the floodgates of delinquent behaviour". And in 2013 a Supreme Court ruling on an earlier challenge to section 377 held that LGBT people constituted a "minuscule minority" who bore only "so-called rights".

In over 40 countries, laws against homosexuality are a lasting legacy of British rule. Unsurprisingly, Britain decriminalized homosexuality in 1967, but, outlandishly, Section 377 stayed in India violating the right to equality enshrined in India's constitution and used as a 'weapon of discrimination'. It was seen as a means to publicly condemn someone's private life, like mine was till this day. The Section came with its share of fear and threat, prison terms, violent bullying, fines and the inevitable social shaming only because people like me, a certain section of the society exercised their sexual preferences.

I had often heard the term "New India", at least two decades ago since India's economic liberalization ensued. Perceptibly, the term has and always will connote different things to different people – an India with potentially the world's largest middle class, a consumer market larger than the entire European Community, a global India with an exploding youth demographic and an ascendant India that can serve as a powerful counter to an intensifying China. Champions of the New India theory, like India's ruling government point to a culture of commanding enterprises and opportunities that have made entrepreneurs of even India's slum dogs. Currently, India is the 6th wealthiest country in the world with a total wealth of $8,230 billion, more than France, Canada, Australia and Italy combined.

The India I see is on the verge of gigantic hormonal changes. India is a fast capitalizing society that has been clocking some fast-paced growth over the past few years and narrates tales of everyday Indians, rustic villages transforming into urban societies and governments coming of age. As the world's fastest-growing major economy, India is poised to displace Germany as the world's 4th-largest economy by 2022 and its economy is expected to grow to $10 trillion from the present $2.3 trillion by 2032. Also, given that we live in the age of neo-liberal capitalism, corporate India can be the instigators of change that make sure working LGBTQ Indians know they are respected and accepted. If most Indian companies become LGBT-friendly, can the rest of the society lag behind?

Over the years, residents have been apprehensive over India's growing problems of dominant governance, corruption and criminalization of politics and escalating political instability. Under India's current able leadership, India is finally reforming and reordering its institutions. Certain chapters like socioeconomics changes, political foundations, developmental and foreign policies are being entirely overwritten to deracinate the momentous changes that India has endured over the last 70 years.

The current government's precursors' concept of secularism as a tool for bringing about socialism was impractical in its denial of all communal identities, like the LGBTQ community, and it was open to abuse by governments. The current government is shattering this impression. India's masses, the youth, the politically conscious, are increasingly participating and are finally finding coherence and direction for political reform and an indigenous model of development.

India today is building itself on self-sustainability, national role models, strengthening the conversation with our tradition and honoring diversity in every walk of life. A strongman leadership, an economic reformer and a populist has transformed lives of millions far afield. Finally, under a dignified powerful leader, India is redefining the definition of India by blending aspirations of the privileged with honorable lives for the under-privileged, irrespective of community, caste or gender.

"History owes an apology to the members of this community and their families... for the ignominy and ostracism that they have suffered through the centuries. They were compelled to live a life full of fear of reprisal and persecution." These were the words by Justice Indu Malhotra, one of the judges of the Indian Supreme Court that ruled against the draconian Section 377 of the IPC.

Always detested by a deeply conservative society, why do we forget that humanity is not confined to male or female? A change in the air is definite. Unlike several other leaders across the globe, our leader is not just tech-savvy, a celebrated storyteller but also governs a culturally tolerant regime that is not hostile to minorities and dissent. He is a global leader with progressive views.

Today I am 40 and my name is Sheila. I have been in a relationship with a man for 3 years. I have a stable job at a prestigious firm in Mumbai. I can finally see achche din! For me, life as a woman is simply a matter of acknowledging my mental state of mind. Since I came out, I have undergone cosmetic surgery and officiated my name and pronoun to the world. Now I am also an advocate of transgender laws and spreading the message of gender-positive identity. The court rulings are a major step towards greater equality that will bring India closer to other jurisdictions across the globe, which are liberalizing laws to make their economies open, welcoming and more inclusive. The rulings represent the emergence of a newer, younger and modern India that is increasingly connected to global ideas including liberal notions of citizenship and rights. Such a ruling will encourage more nations to act soon. It only signals and reinforces how far India has come in a short time to become more accepting of all its citizens.

Under the Pradhan Mantri Awas Yojana that promises grants for home construction, I have applied for a home loan. The dream I have had as a child to own a home, a dream millions merely fantasize about will finally fructify. Our government aims to build, over the next three years, 50 million houses for poor families and is fighting hard to get us there. The fight for greater equality, be it premised on gender, caste, religion, region or sexual orientation, is truly a fight not against law but, against wisdom and old wives' tales that have been passed on to us for generations. I was also reading in a national daily how after Kerala and Odisha, Andhra Pradesh has announced social security pension schemes for the transgender community under which they will be given Rs 1500 per month. I am guessing it is only a matter of time before such schemes are made available pan India. The welfare policies also promise ration cards, housing sites and other financial assistance for business activities, besides scholarships for education and subsidized bus passes.

Yes, education and greater awareness have improved matters, but so insidious are claims pertaining to gays and hijras in India that they continue to hold a certain diabolical resonance in collective consciousness. By attacking such arguments at its very roots, our leaders are reshaping the debate comprehensively. More important is visibility, not just of the sort found in Op-Ed pages and at seminars, but in mass culture. Even Hindi soaps and serials are now steering clear of mind-numbing saas-bahu sagas and focusing on showcasing practical stories that are impacting everyday lives and softening harsh attitudes towards homosexuality.

4 years ago we inherited a crumbling economy. Some harsh actions like what economist Joseph Schumpeter has called "creative destruction" or the "process of industrial mutation that incessantly revolutionises the economic structure from within" has ensured India is back on its track to become a dominant world leader. We have record forex reserves of $415 billion. India climbed 30 ranks in ease of doing business to reach 100th position. Gross FDI inflow has gone up to $61 billion this year.

This Independence Day when our Prime Minister gave his speech, his statement was about resurgent India that did not make a virtue of poverty, instead spelled out measures to alleviate the poverty of millions. He showed impatience to take India ahead of its competitors in both economic and social development. He wasn't coy about India's ambition to be a global leader. He wants India to lead the 4th industrial revolution despite the handicap of his nation missing the previous two and playing catch up in the third.

I can clearly see a new India is rising. It is rising out of the environment-friendly LPG gas stoves of our rural poor households; we have done away with hazardous coal and wood-based cooking for our womenfolk by supplying LPG cylinders to more than 41 million households. It is rising out of the newly electrified remote villages of India; we have electrified all 5, 97,464 villages and 99% urban and 87% rural households in the country. It is rising on the able shoulders of millions of young men and women, especially the SCs and STs; we have extended soft loans to over 70 million of them through Mudra Yojana. A new, confident and well-trained India is rising; out of 20 AIIMS, 22 IITs and 20 IIMs that produce thousands of highly skilled doctors and engineers. We have revolutionised the IT sector through Digital India campaign; the JAM trinity – Jan Dhan, Aadhaar and Mobile – has transformed the lives of ordinary Indians.

My life is an open book. A memoir, a coming-of-age narrative that has irrefutable evidence that I should be understood not by the clothes I wear, not by the name I hold, but through my intellect, undying spirit and wit. According to the new media, although we are an inspiration to millions of people across the world, the transgender movement has definitely come a long way. Nevertheless, the journey ahead is lengthy and arduous. Millions in the LGBTQ community are victims of prejudice and hypocrisy, even to this day. Fortunately, things are taking a turn for the better. Here's to a brighter, more tolerant future.

4

The Moment I Changed My Life Forever – The Day I Started College

I always came first in class. There was no competition. I worked hard, but I would have probably come firstnonetheless. I grasped things quickly, and I possessed a remarkable memory. Teachers often said that for my age, I was one of the sharpest minds they had come across. I enjoyed myself in school, it was always smooth sailing. Unlike the others, there was no subject that I wasn't good at.

My family was extremely proud of me. They narrated tales of my academic successes to whomever they could, and whenever they could. Every time the results were out, they would compare my score with scores of their friends' children. It often seemed as if this comparison was more important to them than my performance, but it never mattered to me, because I always came first. They said that I had inherited my father's intelligence. He too had been just as brilliant when he was young. Ever since I can remember, he has been my inspiration. The way people looked at him, respected his intellect and latched on to his words, was testament to his genius.

But like any other son, I wanted to surpass him too. The feeling was mutual. Like any other father, he wanted me to surpass him. I didn't want to live in his shadow for the rest of my life, and neither did he want me to. I believed that with the scope life offered in this day and age, I could go very far.

My father had grown up in Bhopal, and the schools that he had studied in were quite mediocre. He wasn't from an affluent family. In fact, he told me once that had it not been for certain circumstances, he could have probably been better off in many respects. Back in the day, children had no say in any matter. It was the parents who decided every aspect of their child's life. My grandfather, having observed that my father had an aptitude for the sciences, decided that he would become an engineer. He enrolled him in one of the best engineering colleges of the region. After my father graduated, he forced him to take a job in a government-run firm, for the prevalent belief during those days was that government jobs were the smoothest and steadiest ones. My father still worked for the same company, and we lived with other members of the family in the company quarters.

"I didn't dare speak up or question their decision," he told me. "I should have. I wouldn't have been sitting here for the rest of my life." Having been in a government-run firm for decades, he had witnessed the corruption and the inefficiency first hand. He believed this was a consequence of the country's socialist mindset. "After my graduation, I should have simply made the arrangements and pushed off to the United States," he told me. "I would have had a blooming, intellectually-stimulating career. I would have contributed to the world and made a ton of money at the same time. But there's no point feeling sad now. You must do well and get out of this godforsaken country quickly, I won't impose on you like my father." At that moment I did not notice that he had contradicted himself. What he sought from his children might have been different, but the tendency to impose himself was alive and kicking.

The only difference was that I actually agreed with every word he said. If I had as sharp a mind as they told me, there was no reason not to make the best of it. The most brilliant minds to have emerged out of India in the last few decades did live abroad mostly. And most of the cutting-edge research and breakthroughs did take place in countries like the United States. The fact of the matter was that I wouldn't get much done if, like my father, I too spent the rest of my life in Madhya Pradesh. In those days, we did not even have proper roads, and electricity for 24 hours a day was considered a luxury. To think that there were countries out there where roads and electricity were taken for granted, waiting for third-world talent with open arms, was reassuring.

At an early age, I had it all figured out. I would get into an IIT first, followed possibly by an IIM. After I had successfully graduated from these premier institutions, my life would be set. Multinational companies would roll out the red carpet and vie with each other to have me onboard. I was particularly looking forward to the ones based out of Silicon Valley. Not only were they the most interesting firms, but they generally offered the fattest paychecks too. My parents were delighted. In fact they were more excited about my plan than I was. After all, it was my father who had planted this seed in my mind.

When preparations for the Joint Entrance Exam (JEE) began, I wasn't the only one working hard for it. The entire family began working hard, as if we were all in this together. My cousin used to take me to the tuition centre on his bike, and would often have to pick me up from the centre late at night. My mother stayed up most nights as I prepared, dutifully enquiring if I needed anything to eat or drink every hour. My father, who had the habit of waking up very early in the morning, made sure that I was up early too. Every minute was precious, and I could not afford to miss those morning hours. One a week, my father used to drag the entire family to the temple to pray for me. Divine help had to be sought, we could not take any chances. I wasn't allowed to tag along, for that would mean losing one good hour of preparation time.

At first, I enjoyed this routine. It was a circus, and I was the centrepiece. The attention I received, and the way everyone else's life revolved around me, was quite flattering. Soon, many relatives and friends found out that I was preparing for the JEE. They started keeping a close tab on the preparations, enquiring every now and then about how it was coming along. Whenever I encountered them, they wished me luck. Some of them were candid enough to admit that they had never known anyone who went to an IIT. They asked me not to forget about them when I became 'a big man'. I smiled and politely answered that I had to get into an IIT first, and that I had a long way to go. Did they even know that I was competing for a few hundred seats against lakhs of people across the country?

After returning home from the tuition centre quite late one night, I continued my preparations before finally going to bed in the wee hours of the day. My father religiously woke me up just an hour later, telling me that the morning hours are particularly good for preparations. I was sleep-deprived, I couldn't think clearly. But I dragged myself out of bed, and somehow made it to the desk. My mother walked into the room with a cup of tea. She was dressed in a sari, and had flowers in her hair. She informed me that the family was headed to the temple to pray for me, and that they would be back in an hour. I was dazed still, and I nodded weakly. Soon, everyone had left. My head was aching. I decided to catch a power nap. I would feel fresh again, and I would be up and working by the time they returned.

The next thing I remember is my father shaking me violently. As I opened my eyes, I remember my mother, my cousin, my aunt and other members of the family looking over my father's shoulders, shaking their heads in disapproval. "How could you fall asleep," my father was saying. "How will you ace the exam if you sleep during the day? As a family, we are all making so many sacrifices for you. We go to the temple only to pray for your success! And you're asleep at home?" I sat up on the bed and rubbed my eyes. My father signalled the others to leave the room. Then he turned to me and said, "Son, we're all banking on you. Do you know the sort of prestige that comes along with an IIT degree? Everyone knows you're preparing for this. The entire company quarters, all our friends and relatives, they all know it. You can't let us down, son."

I tried to protest, telling him that I really needed some sleep, and that I was doing my tired brain a favour. He would have none of it. "We have discussed so many times how there is no future here. This is our only chance as a family, son. This is your chance to leave this country for a better life, to ditch a stagnant middle-class for a prosperous future."

That is the moment it dawned on me. I realized why we were all in this together. I was their ticket to a better life. I was the trophy they wanted to show off to the world, that they wanted to dangle before the eyes of their friends and colleagues. But it wasn't as simple as that either. Indeed, they had made several sacrifices, and now their heads were on the line. They had supported me with their time and energy, they had given me everything they could. Now it was all up to me. I had to deliver. There was no room for error. If I didn't deliver, the entire apple cart would come tumbling down. All our efforts would go down in vain. Not just my dreams, ambitions and stature, but those of the entire family depended on how I would fare.

Suddenly, I wasn't enjoying it anymore. The attention and care I received was not flattering now. Every time my family helped me out in any way, it added to the pressure. With each little gesture, I was increasingly compelled to perform. Every time anyone asked me how the preparation was coming along, the list of people whom I had to prove myself kept expanding. I was gradually losing my confidence. The more I thought about the future, the more nervous I felt. To top it off, nobody seemed to understand that I had physical limitations. I required a few hours of sleep every day to keep my mind fresh. But their insecurity was turning me into a zombie. I could sense that unlike when I had started, I was taking much more time to process things.

I missed getting into an IIT by 12 ranks. Considering how tough and competitive it is, missing it by just 12 ranks is an achievement by itself. But most people don't see things that way. Overnight, the mood at home changed. People were not sympathetic at all. Everyone's dreams had come crumbling down, and they held me responsible for it. They made no effort to hide it. I was shattered. Not only had I let myself down, but I had let down the entire family. I would never move abroad now, things would always remain the same. And how would my parents show their faces to our neighbours, our relatives, and our friends? Now, they would forever be the parents of that boy who tried to make it to IIT but failed.

I just lay in bed the entire day, crying. Nobody was by side. Everyone seems to be too disappointed themselves to bother about me, or too angry to even look at my face. Nobody called me outside for lunch, not that I cared for lunch that day. What would I do with my life now? There was literally nothing left for me to do. This had been the plan all along. I had failed, and there was no alternate plan. In the evening, my cousin finally came into my room. He looked disturbed, as if I had deprived him of something. He told me, "All those tuitions didn't help you at all. Your father kept asking you to work harder… Anyway. I don't know what you will do with your life now." He sat at the foot of the bed for a while and looked at me pitifully. Then he stood up and left.

It's one thing to wonder what you're going to do with your life, and quite another to know that the rest of the world is wondering the same thing. It confirms your suspicion that you're good for nothing. It breaks you. It makes you feel hollow and useless. I thought I had wasted my life. I felt it wasn't worth living anymore. Day after day, I lay in bed contemplating suicide. My family was gradually moving on with their lives. I saw them only during mealtimes, and they maintained a stone-cold silence. The pain that I had caused to them was palpable. I knew that day was not far when I would either jump down from the third floor or consume poison.

My father one day walked into my room and broke down. I didn't quite understand what was happening. When he had calmed down, he finally told me that he hated seeing me like this. He told me that not getting into an IIT was not the end of the world, and that with such a great rank, any NIT in the country would be happy to have me. He said, "It took some time for me to come to terms with the fact that we had pushed you too hard. Our expectations were unrealistic." He informed me that he had already sent in several applications to various NITs on my behalf, and that we would hear from them soon. "This doesn't change anything," he told me. "You're bright and hardworking. Nothing in the world will stop your resolve."

Very soon, I packed my bags and headed to NIT Delhi. I had decided that I would stop daydreaming about the future. I would give my best, and hope for the best. I had nothing to lose, and no reason to live in sorrow. The moment I returned to the classroom, I got my old mojo back. This was my territory. I began grasping subjects quickly once again. My performance was strong and consistent. And most importantly, I was regaining my psychological balance. I felt healthy and confident, ready to take on the world.

During my time in NIT, a lot changed across the country. When my mother called me up, she often spoke about how power cuts had stopped completely back home. In Delhi, I noticed a lot of change first hand. As an engineering graduate, it was an instructive experience. Clogged, pot-holed roads were turning into swanky new highways, and the metro was making every corner of the city accessible within minutes. But what really struck me were the technological changes. We received super-fast 4G internet for a fraction of what we used to shell out for 3G connections. Soon, I was making all my payments from the phone. Delicious food from any part of the city could be delivered to our hostel's doorstep. I could stand anywhere and hail a reasonably-priced cab within seconds. This is how my life was becoming increasingly convenient, and I realized how technology was empowering millions across the country.

For the first time, I began to look at India differently. It was no longer a non-serious, inefficient country that was doomed to fail. I saw it as a country on the move, a land of unending potential. Reading about how the country was using cutting edge technology to deliver services to people became one of my favourite past-times. Through Aadhar, the government was taking the help of biometrics to ensure that subsidies reached the poor, and that there were no leakages in the way. Through Digital India, government services were gradually becoming available online. Not just as an engineer but as a keen observer of the world, it was a great time to be India. We were in transition.

As the end of my course approached, I was finally compelled to think of my next course of action. It was great to see the country in transition, but I was still toying with the idea of a career abroad. Other countries offered a larger scope for research, and more financial stability. That's when I came across this new scheme called the Prime Minister Research Fellowship that the government had conceived of. I soon realized that it was aimed at people like me. Unlike in the past when they just didn't care, they wanted us to use our talent right here instead of doing it on foreign soil.

The scheme was cleverly designed. Three thousand fellows would be selected in the first round, and would be enrolled to PhD programmes at premier institutions. There, they would have to conduct cutting-edge research in science and technology, but with a special focus on national priorities. They would be given massive grants as well. Starting at seventy thousand rupees per month, it would gradually increase to eighty thousand rupees by the fifth year. Contingency expenses of two lakh rupees would also be granted every year. The fellows would have to teach at neighbouring colleges too. The scheme would serve three purposes simultaneously. The most obvious one is that it would arrest the ongoing brain-drain. Additionally, if some of the brightest minds focused on projects of national importance, one can only imagine the edge it would give to India. And lastly, it would ensure quality faculty for the students in the neighbourhood.

As the deadline to present my project abstract for the scheme approaches, I am working day and night on the proposal. My research, if the distinguished screening committee accepts, will be in the domain of solar panels. I believe there are ways of making these panels more cost-efficient and energy-efficient. Environment-friendly policies are not only the need of the hour, but something that India is pursuing steadfastly. I cannot wait to be part of the great India story. Finally, our country is giving its brightest minds a chance to succeed. Staying back in the country, and being part of the change, seems like a much more satisfying prospect today. And believe it or not, the person encouraging me the most to follow this path, is my father.

5. I Broke Barriers, Tore Apart Stereotypes: The Day I Turned Entrepreneur

I come from a traditional family in Jaisalmer where, by the time you are 18 and have no plans for further studies, you have to get married and take care of your family. That's the implicit norm, every woman under her foot-long *ghunghat* has to abide by. Rural Indian women like my mother and her ancestors have never had much by way of social agency or power to formulate strategic choices, control resources and take decisions that affect important life outcomes.

Despite pre-natal sex determination being banned in India, when my mother conceived me, not my parents, not my grandparents, but the elderly conformist women in my village had forced my mother to undergo a gender identification test. If it was a girl, they would kill it in the womb, she had no values to add to the family. If it was a boy, they would let my mother bear the child, they were getting their rightful heir after-all! When they came to know it was a girl-child, they were up in arms against my family to get the pregnancy terminated. Fortunately, my parents fought back with all their might. Mine was once a state where girls were killed every day, with the worst statistics of female infanticide in India. Rajasthan, the land of *samman* and *parampara*, was also the land of *sharm* and *dar*. In my town, men preferred to keep their women behind veils, while their daughters were buried deep inside graves.

I come from a place where child marriage was once a rampant practice, villages notorious for dowry deaths and a place where girls were once born to die. India is home to the largest number of child brides in the world. According to recent estimates, 47% of girls in India are still married away before they reach 18. I was fortunate. My best friend Meena wasn't. Meena was married off at the age of 13 to a man 15 years older to her. Next year, Meena became pregnant, and her child and she died during childbirth. Even today, when I think of Meena and her unborn child, shivers run down my spine.

Things are, however, changing, thanks to crusaders who are fighting against child marriages and associated predicaments. There also are advocates of rights like my parents who are silently hauling Rajasthan out of its gloomy and miserable facade. People are familiar with Rajasthan as seen in movies with its incredible imagery – and indeed, Rajasthan is all that: stunning palaces, forts, havelis and gorgeous desert landscapes. But, it's much more intense than what meets the eyes. At the ground level, there are revolutions ensuing in every village that stood neglected so far. Women are successfully overcoming deep-seated cultural resistance to catalyze change. As the saying by French writer, poet and politician Alphonse de Lamartine goes, "There is a woman at the beginning of all great things" and women of Rajasthan are proving it right through their deeds. They have accomplished enormous strides in their careers and are proudly walking alongside their male counterparts in bringing great glory to their names.

When I was growing up, the villagers ostracized my parents for sending me to school, something that was a taboo for a girl child. *"Padai karke kya karna? Pati ko khilana pilana hai or bachche paida karne hai!"* they use to taunt. Village elders ridiculed my parents for having an unmarried daughter at home. I was a 'burden', not surprisingly for my parents, but for the village at large. My mother had always been one all her life, a burden on the family she was born into, married at the age of 14 so that she could care for her real family.

Once, my mother had told me something so stirring, it has been etched on my mind since. She had told me, "Know your self-worth, identify your strengths to chase your dreams and always know how truly and deeply I love you. Live with a purpose, love without fear, dream with passion and live a life without regret." Her words, inspiring, fervent, heartening and cheerful have left an indelible mark on my life. I was blessed to have got this life. I had to make it worth living for. I had to be different. I chose to be different.

In a male dominated, tremendously chauvinistic society, women across India are breaking barriers, undertaking roles that have always been "mardon ka kaam". From sarpanches of India's remote villages to feisty truck drivers, from world champion players from some of India's innermost hamlets to revered police personnel, women are daring to break the mould and taking on unconventional career paths, professions that would have been frowned upon just a few years ago. Stories of dedicated women revolutionizing societal norms with grassroots leadership in making a difference in a country plagued by corruption and inefficiency are making headlines worldwide. Development experts too have widely recognized women's contribution to village leadership as critical to economic progress, healthy civil society and good governance in India.

And why not? The transformations that India is witnessing today are monumental, revolutions that she has waited to see for a very long time. The dream of building a new India is only possible when women are empowered and their true potential is unleashed by providing them opportunities in society and financial decision making. However, words are futile if they are not backed by actions. Following up ideas and ideals with actions is of prime importance and our leaders are leading the way. They may look trivial, but with gestures like making cooking smoke-free for over 3 crore women in India, building toilets in over 6 crore households, our leaders are ensuring that the dignity and health of women are not tarred anymore. This is a culture that embodies true and irreversible empowerment, not mere handouts right before elections.

Chhavi Rajawat, one of India's youngest sarpanches, a one-woman army who sought to drag her impoverished ancestral village in the desert state of Rajasthan into the 21st Century had always been my role model. Armed with an MBA, if she could quit her plush corporate career to change the face of a village, so could I. Studies published in various journals show that living in a village that had elected a female leader or a sarpanch caused villagers to report lower bias against women. By creating empowered female role models, they also led villagers to state higher aspirations for their daughters and to invest more in their education.

I have always believed in one thing – the difference between successful people and others is how long they spend time feeling sorry for themselves for not having done something worth with their lives. I was born to break the glass ceiling and prove myself fearless while standing up against societal taboos and work towards women empowerment. When I was a child, there was one thing that I knew and that was to not being a submissive housewife. I was determined to build a skill-set, equip myself with values and add worth to my sheer existence. I knew, location was no barrier for ambition!

As I grew older, so did my aspirations. I started brewing different plans. I wanted to become a wedding planner. Here was my amusing yet factual take on weddings in India. No matter what the season, no matter how the economy is doing, no matter what caste or religion you belong to, grand, glitzy and extravagant weddings will take place. Indian weddings are week long affairs that are dramatic and grand to say the least. Multinational conglomerates were tapping into this lucrative industry, pegged at an all-time high of 50 billion dollars, and centering their products on it, why couldn't I?

A little back in time, things in the wedding industry weren't what they look now. It was micro managed with separate units working on the end product. It was a family affair where everybody from distant uncles to close cousins chipped in to make the marriage ceremonies successful. However, over the past couple of years, the event management industry particularly wedding planning department has undergone drastic changes making the field competitive, creative, fun, challenging and methodical. I knew this, I had to show this to the world.

With a larger-than-life dream on one hand, I realized I had no money on the other to get started. My parents were my anchor. My father introduced me to a yojana that was providing funding to the non-corporate, non-farm sector. In a nation that needs to empower its women more than ever, plans such as these are trying their best to improve the status of the 'fairer, weaker sex' by providing them with small loans, encouraging them to start new ventures and in turn empower them by allowing them to attain financial security and stability and become self-governing. Swami Vivekananda had once said, "The idea of perfect womanhood is perfect independence." Women are enterprising; they don't need to be taught. All they need is opportunities to perform. Independence makes a woman assertive and empowered and empowered women are a "bulwark against societal evils".

Like most young women, at first, I was skeptical and wary of government schemes because of the tedious bureaucracy and paperwork involved. However, a seamless process fetched me a loan of 5 lakhs in no time and I embarked on my journey. Shattering all labels aside, my mother served as my manager, my father helped me get raw materials from bigger cities like Jaipur, Bikaner, Ajmer and Udaipur. When 2 young girls in my village were pushed into child marriage, I took them under my wings and in doing so, I gave them the might to fight against such carnages. They were creative and driven, the only two qualities I needed for a job like this, qualities these young talented girls possessed in abundance.

Small-scale businesses were previously unsupported by banks and acquiring a loan for the same was a struggle. As per a report by GEDI, globally 73% Indian women failed to get funding from venture capitalists and India ranked among the last five in the list of 30 countries studied. The Mudra scheme supports more than 50 million small business owners, a majority of which are women. The scheme also simplifies repayment of loans by eliminating middle-men and bringing entrepreneurs and financial institutions onto a single platform. In a fast-growing economy where gender parity in the workforce is amongst the lowest in the world, this move empowers women to take charge of their financial independence and be an equal and assertive participant in the nation's workforce.

When words like "Women empowerment is vital to India's development" are voiced at prestigious congresses like the Global Entrepreneurship Summit by a man, it gives hope to millions of aspirational women from every walk of life, who have harbored dreams of being an active participant in India's workforce. Our government has time and again sent clear, strong signals that it's high time women are adequately represented in the country's economic and political domains. Several policies and developmental measures have been put in place to give wings to the dreams and ambitions of women entrepreneurs, who in turn, will become job-creators and empower other women in their communities.

India is also a nation which is marred by undernourishment, especially in and around rural villages. This menace, starvation, has been killing lakhs every year. India has vowed to end malnutrition by 2022 and experts have reason to believe that women empowerment can be one of the ways in which India will win this battle. It's correct right? Women have a decision-making role in households and empowering them can influence her decisions. This could result in the fulfillment of nutritional needs of the family.

I have signed up with the Startup India program where the signing on process was quick and efficient and my loan was approved within no time, along with the 25% subsidy for the term capital and other benefits such as subsidized electricity. I am now in the process of finishing my entrepreneur development program organized by the EDI and have already booked workstations in other cities across Rajasthan.

I am also in talks with an NGO for the training and employment of transgenders in my firm. All my raw materials are sourced from local farmers and small businesses with the tag that proudly broadcasts Made in India. According to the 6th Economic Census, out of the 58.5 million entrepreneurs in India, 8.05 million are women. Women constitute 13.76% of the total entrepreneurs in the country and they provide employment to 13.45 million people.

The success and transformation that Beti Bachao Beti Padhao has brought, both in attitudes and in outcomes, will be remembered fondly by history. Under Swachh Vidyalaya, my school saw separate toilets for girls and boys, a step that has drastically reduced girls dropping out of schools. Mudra and Jan Dhan have brought formal financial inclusion and entrepreneurial opportunities to crores of women like me. With the preponderance of women in positions of power, like never seen before, women know that there is no domain that they cannot enrich and there are no barriers that can ever stop them.

Digitalisation and skilling initiatives are blessings for women who have never received conventional vocational education or had to drop out of school/college for various reasons. Even in the absence of schooling and traditional academic or vocational qualifications, millions of women now have an opportunity to acquire skills and training which will empower them to earn an independent living. New India is not about eradicating a nation and starting from scratch, it is about giving them opportunities so that they can rightfully express their innate leadership qualities. Women possess commanding qualities like excellent management abilities, communication skills and ability to multitask. When they are given a free rein to, India will shine. For a little girl in a remote village, new India is the place where she stands an equal chance to lead the nation as much as her brothers do. This is not just women empowerment but women-led development.

Backed by the myriad schemes missioned towards boosting the Indian startup ecosystem and empowering women, I have come a long way in my road of self-discovery. Today, I have 25 women working with me on my out of the ordinary venture. With the remuneration I give them, not only has their lives become easier and more convenient, it has also contributed to a marked increase in their productivity. They are able to tend to their homes and families in a much healthier way. I could not have achieved more happiness and most importantly, my parents could not be prouder. My father proudly proclaims, *"Meri beti, 10 mardo jaisi!"* Financial independence forms the foundation of women empowerment and things in this sphere are changing fast and for the better. In the coming years, I plan to employ more women from my community and scale up my business operations. With a nation that has been marred by unemployment, entrepreneurs have been welcomed with open arms. I have been able to generate manifold employment opportunities for several and have been able to convince foreign VCs to invest in my business thus creating ripples of success through my disruptive idea that's boosting economic growth.

Revolutions bring changes in a day but reforms take time. In a country where the agenda of women empowerment has largely been neglected since Independence, it is heartening to see that policies are now being put in place to propel women towards emancipation. Empowering women economically and otherwise is a Herculean task, but the arduous journey in this direction has already begun. It's only a matter of time before we see these efforts bear fruit and our country becoming a truly developed nation with robust participation from the womenfolk.

5

I Chose To Marry At 35! The Society Empowered Me To

I am from Assam, a state where weddings are humble and rooted with one-of-a-kind rituals that are profoundly entrenched in traditions. As a child, I had grown up believing that marriage was an important part of a woman's life merely because that's how she identified herself in the society, as someone's wife, as Mrs. My mother, the quintessential housewife, had done that all her life. Glamorous Hindi cinemas with romanticized versions of marriage influenced me. All my cousins were married soon after they finished college. I knew my day would come soon.

However, as I grew older, I realized the harsh reality behind getting girls married off early. Men wanted "virgin" brides and it was far easier for parents to get young girls married off than monitor them, confine them and what if they fell in love with someone "unworthy", which in turn would make them "undeserving"? They would bring enormous shame and dishonor to the entire family. Girls who failed to get married young were looked down upon by the prying neighbors and society lords. They were instantly condemned, indicted and declared unworthy marriage material. What was their fault? They weren't married at the age the society wanted them to, that's all. What was even more horrific was that the same people sniggered even more if a woman wished to marry late as if with advancing age they were not worthy of marital bliss and companionship! "Having babies will be a problem", "People will think you are not adjusting enough" and even worse, "Society will think you are a divorcee or something" were labels that inevitably came attached.

We are well into the 21st century, hurtling towards a new era, a new revolution in science and technology, but women in India and certain conformist communities across the globe still struggle. As soon as they step into their 20s, they have to deal with the pressure of getting married to a 'suitable' man. I believe there are many things wrong with this belief. First, it assumes that every woman is interested in men. Second, it assumes that every woman wants to get married. Third, the pressure on men to be 'suitable' is a completely different ball game.

Marital rape, a grave, yet widespread form of violence against women in India is also highly predominant. According to the National Family Health Survey, 29% of women between 15 and 49 years of age said they had faced physical or sexual violence at the hands of their husbands. With this exception, are we reinforcing the patriarchal notion that a woman's body is her husband's property?

Sadly, there were double standards when it came to the boys of my family. All my *dadas* were often told to wait to get married until they felt ready – until they were mature, financially secure, established in their careers and comfortable with themselves. My own *dada* was counseled by my parents numerous times to not even consider marriage until he was 35 years old. He took their advice to the next level and married at 40. He was praised and his measured and mature decision was applauded. Somehow, even our movies and soaps had been convincing generations that if they didn't marry in their childbearing years, it would never happen.

Thankfully, today, such disparities between girls and boys are being bridged. Finding a husband to ensure their future is secure is no longer the biggest priority for women. Increasingly, they are opting for professional success over early conjugal life which is why many women are now marrying later in life. India's External Affairs Minister, Defence Minister and the Speaker of the Indian Parliament, three of the most prestigious ranks there are, are helmed by women. The changing stature of the Indian woman is evident. They are storming corporate citadels and altering the urban workforce landscape, reaping laurels for the nation. As India sprints to attain its Sustainable Development Goals for gender equality and women's empowerment, women are marching ahead in the race. Like they say, empowerment begins at home. It begins by drawing out women – mothers, sisters, maids, grandmothers, who have never expressed their dreams, desires or problems. You are never 'too old' to be empowered.

Marriage was once simply marked as the passing of economic stewardship from a woman's father to her background-checked husband. But as more women join the workforce in India and become economically independent, the meaning of marriage has drastically changed. I was one of them. Like *Mr. Charles M Blow had once said, "There is no wrong time to do the right thing!"*

Armed with an MSc, I was working at a prestigious firm in New Delhi and was home for vacations. A straight A grade student all my life, I wasn't content. Something inside me was amiss. I knew that in order to achieve something significant and to improve my skill set, I had to team my MSc with a PhD. My study playing field was one-off. I have always been fascinated by quantum science and technology, thus electing photonics was an unquestionable decision. Whilst I was ransacking website after website to select a PhD program that would offer me what I desired, my nosy neighbors were busy brewing stories of my marriage, something I wasn't even thinking of. Marriage is amazingly tenacious, this cliché: women see the institution as a protection, men see it as a constraint. Women long for it and men evade it; women fantasise about it while men hope that if they keep their heads down, it won't come up. It's a well-told myth: a woman over a certain age has a better chance of getting struck by lightning than finding a mate. Funny, isn't it?

My quest for finding a PhD program finally ended. I was ready to head to Vancouver. Luckily, when I'd delivered this message to my parents, they were super supportive and not the least worried that I was already in my early 30s and still single. I've been privileged enough to have parents who have given me the freedom to make my own choices, but that doesn't stop others from *worrying* over my single status. In India, the marriage market is literally a combat zone. A potential bride could be rejected for anything: being chubby, being dark skinned, being too 'old', inability to cook, love for meat, modern ideas, wears jeans, even 'too much education.' As a liberated young woman, I was so over-zealous about my personal and financial independence, that when it came to marriage, I would not compromise my life for the institution, at least not right at the moment. The life my mother had chosen for herself. Despite getting a well-regarded job as a lecturer at a University in New Delhi, she had to quit in order to move to Assam with her husband, my father when he got transferred. She had no choice. My father would not, she had to. For me on the other hand, a good man is not a good retirement plan.

Our government, the leaders we have elected are trailblazers in leading the way to women empowerment. The vision we have of a New India by 2022 is only possible if women, the fairer sex are allowed to advance. Women should be free to choose, whether it is their career, education, marriage or having a family.

It was during my PhD at Vancouver that I met my future husband. I was 32, what is traditionally considered well past "marriageable age" in India. It's never too late to get married, but it can always be too early. An Indian by birth, Naren had lived in Vancouver all his life. He was past 40 and was still resolutely happily unmarried. I wanted a connection that was an equal partnership, one in which I could pursue my passions and career with his support. Here's something about love my grandma had once told me, "What doesn't happen in years, happens in minutes". I was 35 when we finally decided to tie the knot in a traditional ceremony back home. By then, I had completed my PhD and had co-founded an e-commerce company alongside Naren.

I wanted to come to India and start a new venture on the same lines. After all, India's retail ecommerce sales is set to climb 31% this year to reach $32.70 billion, trailing only China and Indonesia in Asia-Pacific. By 2022, 41.6% of the Indian population will be digital shoppers owing to India's rising internet and smartphone use, as well as the country's youth populace and expanding middle class. Foreign investments, a critical driver of economic growth and a major source of non-debt financial resource for the economic development of India are at an all-time high. FDI investments in India in the 2nd quarter of 2018 stood at US$ 12.75 billion indicating that our government's relentless efforts to improve ease of doing business and relaxation in FDI norms is yielding significant results.

When I conveyed my decision of getting married in India and in addition also founding a company, my parents were very encouraging. Even my neighbors who were once highly inquisitive of my affairs had mellowed. My age, my weight and my ability to bear children, some concerns that become a matter of intense scrutiny in the marriage market were thrown out of the window. I got married in a low key affair because I was more inclined towards starting my business rather than pumping more money into the already flourishing Rs 100,000 crore Indian wedding market that is rapidly growing at a 25 to 30% rate annually. Indian weddings are gala occasions to say the least.

Marriage, a union is about synergy and striking a new balance. Being a couple means that the needs, wants and desires of both individuals are acknowledged. You can always be a power couple and still have your own individuality. You don't need to lose your independence or put brakes on your success simply because you are married. You should be loved and respected for all of that.

Only, over the last 2 years, an employment generation programme has helped women entrepreneurs across India set up 30,437 projects with financial assistance of over Rs 853 crore. Several portals, platforms and yojanas are being initiated regularly to encourage women entrepreneurs to protect their interests and upskill themselves. Empowering women to participate fully in economic life across all sectors is essential to building stronger economies, achieve internationally agreed goals for development and sustainability and generally improve the quality of life for families and communities. When I came back to Assam after 5 years, it was an eye-opening sight to witness girls going to schools, on account of schemes that have been aiming to promote educational opportunities among girl students and address the challenges of lower girl enrolment rates in educational institutions. Platforms that empower girl students and provides them with better learning opportunities are a welcome change in a nation that was once notorious for vanquishing its girls to domestic violence and child marriage.

When I started my business, I had pledged to devote myself to the wellbeing of the nation and the service of the poor. I knew that the challenges women face is vastly different from what men face. It is not just about taking care of the household, they invariably take a break from work because of marriage and children. But, once they get back, there is a massive gap in the skills they possess and the accelerating market. I hired an all-women force to steer my business. With their excellent managerial and entrepreneurial skills, women have enormous capacity to raise the standard of living in towns and Tier II cities like mine. Marriage or having children was not going to stop them, it did not.

Sometime back, a crisp, comprehensive and concise document had caught my attention. In 1941, Bapu, Mahatma Gandhi had written the 'Constructive Programme: Its meaning and place' which he had subsequently modified in 1945, when there was renewed fervor around the freedom movement. He had in detail touched upon a wide range of topics ranging across rural development, strengthening agriculture, enhancing sanitation, promoting Khadi, empowerment of women, economic equality among other issues. It was an eye-opening essay. Why can't we make this our guiding light and build an India of Bapu's dreams? The subjects he had deliberated upon then are absolutely relevant today and whilst our government is trying to fulfil as many it can, it's our responsibility, the citizens of India to work towards a new India.

Over the last four years, 130 crore Indians have paid tributes to Mahatma Gandhi in the form of the Swachh Bharat Mission, something that's clearly evident in my town. It's no more a scheme, a plan on paper, it has emerged as a pulsating mass movement that has witnessed commendable outcomes across the nation. Over 85 million households now have access to toilets for the first time. Over 400 million Indians no longer have to defecate in the open. In a short span, sanitation coverage is up from 39% to 95%. Twenty-one states, Union territories and 4.5 lakh villages are now open defecation free. One of Mahatma Gandhi's favourite chants was "Vaishnav jan to tene kahiye je, peer parayee jaane re," which signifies "a good soul is one who feels the pain of others." It was this spirit that made him live for others. Today, we, the 1.3 billion Indians are committed to working together to fulfil the dreams Bapu had once envisioned for the country he gave his life for.

6

They Say That You Only Become A Mother When You Give Birth. I Beg To Differ.

Ever since I can remember, I was extremely diligent. In my entire student-life, I was as hard-working as they came. And after that, when I got a job, I was completely career-oriented. It did not matter if I had to stay up late to finish work, it did not matter if I had to go in on weekends sometimes. In fact, I quite enjoyed it. I was a workaholic. Some of us are like that, we don't quite know what to do with our free time if there is no work.

People often told me that I had no life outside of work, and that I should do something about it. I never felt the need to. I guess some people don't feel the need to have a family, to have a large friend circle, or to spend the weekend in meaningless socializing. They wished to impose their standards on me, but I would have none of it.

My parents were quite happy at first. Why would any parent be unhappy about raising a serious and hard-working girl who was least bothered with superficial banalities? At some point, they did get a bit concerned. You cannot blame them. I had an unusually small friend circle, and it was only when I worked that I was really in my element. But I explained to them that this is how I like it. It wasn't that I was averse to people. I just preferred engaging myself constantly, learning, making an effort, getting things done. They finally understood.

It all began on my thirtieth birthday. I was a senior executive at a multinational company by then, and several of the company's projects were completely dependent on me. I had acquired a reputation of delivering, and so the most crucial projects always came my way. It was almost impossible to take any time off, and I liked to keep things that way. My parents though had begged me to take that day off for months. After all, your thirtieth birthday is a special birthday. I would have liked nothing better than to spend the day working for sixteen hours, but I obliged. My parents never asked for much, and this was the least I could do.

My mother had prepared an elaborate meal of the things I loved. My father had woken up early and driven down to the other end of the city to get a cake from my favourite bakery. They just wanted to spend the day chatting with me and having a great time, since they hardly got a chance to do it. It was a lovely day. They finally understood, in detail, what I did at work. I heard some funny stories from my childhood. We exchanged views on various issues. We enjoyed ourselves thoroughly. I took them out to dinner at a fancy restaurant. I can't describe the look on their faces on our way back that night. I had never seen them so happy, so satisfied. I told them, and they were both of the opinion that it's the effect your children can have on you.

It didn't mean much at first, but it got me thinking. Work was what filled me with joy, but perhaps there were other joys that I hadn't experienced. I remembered the look on my father's face everyday when I came out of school. I remember the look on my mother's face each time I told her how well I had done in the exam, or that I had received a promotion at work. Pure, unadulterated joy. The joy of simply watching the most precious person in your life grow, learn and evolve. It was something I had never experienced. And suddenly, I wanted to.

Before that moment, the only other time I had done anything for a child was to sponsor the education of an underprivileged girl. One of my colleagues had told me about an NGO through which one could do this, and she had been doing it for a year. Without thinking too much, I too began sponsoring a child. I was doing well, and I was making much more money than I needed. I had no family of my own, and I had no time for expensive shopping or luxurious holidays. It was the least I could do. I would be told how she was faring every once in a while. I did not have to meet her or speak with her. It was a format that suited me. But what I wanted now was much more than that. I didn't just want to throw money and feel good about it, I wanted to be intimately involved.

I was thirty, and the idea of starting a family had never occurred to me. I was not in a position to throw away a thriving career that I had painstakingly built. And I did not have the time or the energy to go out there, find Mr. Perfect and start a family. That isn't how I wanted to go about it anyway. I began weighing my options, and there seemed to be only one solution.

The problem with that solution was that many people in India did not think very highly of it. It was considered the last choice. It was considered to be a sign of infertility. You must have guessed by now. I wanted to adopt. When I told my parents about it, they were delighted. A practice that many from their generation might have considered taboo, was embraced by them. They told me unequivocally that they would support me completely, and that they were eagerly waiting for their new grandchild to join the family. My mother had tears in her eyes. That's the day I realized that she had wanted a grandchild more than anything, but that out of sheer consideration for me, she had suppressed that wish for years.

Not everyone accepted my decision so easily though. Some of my colleagues were unsure, and brought to my notice all the baggage that comes with adoption. But I was determined. I knew that the respectable existence of single mothers in India was something we were still coming to terms with, but I was ready to face any challenge that came my way. After all, if someone did not stand up and prove to the world that what I was about to do was completely normal, how would things change? It was because of people who had broken stereotypes that homosexuality, the acceptance for the girl child, the acceptance for transgenders and other such social breakthroughs were slowly becoming the norm.

I knew that I would have to make certain sacrifices, and I prepared myself for them. It wouldn't be business as usual. I wouldn't be able to work for sixteen hours a day, and I would have to take the weekends off. I wasn't going to do this in a half-hearted way. I informed my boss about the decision I had taken. He hadn't expected this, but he congratulated me and expressed how happy he was for me. I must admit that I was not a hundred percent prepared to give up on the intense career-oriented life that I lived until I went to the adoption centre.

It was a life altering experience. She was asleep in her crib, with her head turned away from us. I turned her gently towards us to get a glimpse of her face. It woke her up. Half asleep, her first impulse was a smile, the most beautiful I had ever seen. When I carried her in my arms, I soon realized how in such a short span of time, my daughter had trusted me. She had trusted me despite the fact that I was a complete stranger to her. Walking out of the adoption centre with my daughter in my arms and my excited parents following closely, I realized that I had become a mother.

There was no looking back after this. My daughter had begun recognizing me on our first day together. The moment she woke up, her eyes would search the room until they found me. Immediately, she would break into a smile. I sat next to her for hours when she slept, waiting for her to wake up. My parents were over the moon. They reached out to every relative, and every friend of theirs, and shared the news with them. Our neighbours, especially the children, often came home to play with my daughter.

Some people in my parents' social circles were aghast. In retrospect, it was comical. When my parents told them I had a daughter now, they were livid about not having been invited to my wedding and not knowing that I was expecting a child. My parents had to explain to them that none of that really happened, and that my daughter was adopted. They asked my parents if everything was alright with me, and why I had not chosen the conventional route to have a child. My parents explained to them that this is how I had chosen to do things, and that it was quite alright.

But some of them were not easily convinced. For them, my parents had to use the example of Sita. King Janak and his wife Sunaina were childless, and they found Sita in a field. She became the centre of their world. In fact, according to several accounts, she was even dearer to her father than Urmila, the daughter that the royal couple later had. The other example my parents used was that of Satyavati. Having grown up with a fisherman who found her as a little baby, she married king Shantanu of Hastinapur and went on to play an important role in the events that led to the battle of Kurukshetra. These examples could not be refuted even by the most narrow-minded of people. Slowly but surely, my decision was accepted by everyone.

A week after bringing my daughter home, it was time to go back to work. A part of me was looking forward to it. I could not remember the last time I had spent an entire week not working at all. But for the first time, another part of me did not feel like getting back. She was so tiny, and I loved her so much. How could I leave her at home and go to work? I knew my parents would take good care of her, that they would go out of their way to ensure that she was looked after. But leaving the house that morning is the toughest thing I have done in my life. I checked and cross-checked several things with my parents, just to ensure that they were fully equipped. They answered patiently and reassuringly. They reminded me that they had raised a child, and that they knew exactly what they were doing.

My colleagues were delighted to see me. Work had taken a beating without me. The clients were livid, and wanted to know when I would return. My boss was overworked, and he looked like he hadn't slept for days. He heaved a sigh of relief when he saw me. He smiled and said that things would finally be back on track. I got to work immediately. It felt great. But very soon, I remembered that it had been more than an hour since I had left home. I called my parents. I could hear my daughter crying in the background. They told me that she missed me, but that things were under control. I could not concentrate. I could not think clearly. My mind kept returning to my daughter.

By lunchtime, I had made three calls already. It had been terribly difficult to pacify her. She was fast asleep by then, and my parents were catching a break. My mother had been unable to cook lunch, and she was quickly assembling some sandwiches. I felt terrible. In the afternoon, my boss called me to his cabin. He seemed unusually flustered, and I could see him trying to control himself. I had known him for a long time, and I knew he liked me for the work that I did. He spoke to me quite honestly, telling me that some of the work I had sent out in the morning was rather hurried. He told me that I had never submitted such sub-standard work in the past, and that he was genuinely concerned. Having grown quite close to him through the years, I was able to tell him quite honestly what the matter was.

He heard me out patiently and nodded. He had guessed as much. When I finished speaking, he asked me if I was aware of the Maternity Benefit Amendment Act, which had come into effect just the previous year. I shook my head, not quite knowing which direction he was taking this to. "For your peace of mind, you must bring her here every day. Every organization with more than fifty employees is mandatorily required to provide a crèche facility. If you need it, we will provide it. It's as simple as that." I felt as if a huge burden had just been lifted off my chest. It was almost as if that scheme had been designed especially for me. I was overjoyed. I thanked him profusely. "Don't thank me," he said. "The law is the law."

When I returned to my desk, I decided to do my own research, just to be sure. I did not want to celebrate prematurely. What if the management simply shot down my boss' proposal on some technical ground? I found out that they could not do that. It wasn't really up to them. The government had drafted strict guidelines in this regard. Since they employed over three thousand people across the country, and over two hundred at our facility itself, they were well within the ambit of those guidelines. A crèche would be up and running soon, and my daughter would be the first member. I would not have to worry about her since she would be a stone throw away the whole day. There would be professional help taking care of her. If I was needed, I could be there in a matter of seconds. I could spend lunch break with her, and check on her every once in a while. And most importantly, my parents who were both senior citizens now would not have to stress about her.

While doing my research about the Maternity Benefit Amendment Act, I learned about its purpose and what its implications were. It was quite fascinating. This act of course made headlines for being revolutionary because it mandated twelve weeks of maternity leave in India. But provisions like having a crèche at any workplace with more than fifty employees ensured that a new mother would not have to forego her career due to childbirth. Women would now remain in the workforce. Their careers would not suffer setbacks which popped up in the past only due their gender.

But what if an organisation had less than fifty employees, I wondered? In fact, most organisations probably have less than fifty employees. Many of them are small and medium industries, and their workforce is largely made up of the aspiring class. Would new mothers who worked at smaller firms and who were not as fortunate as I was, not be able to avail of this scheme? Our policymakers must have noticed this obvious gap, and are now working towards covering it. An old scheme has been revived to help women in need. The Rajiv Gandhi National Crèche Scheme is now being implemented on the ground with new guidelines. Working mothers with children in between the age of six months and six years can leave their children at these crèches during the day. They will be operated by local NGOs, and will run for 26 days a month.

This makes me very happy. Many women from across the spectrum will benefit from this. I still remember how I felt the day I had to get back to work. Such an overwhelming feeling might have prompted many women not to return to work. But we are finding solutions to the problem. We are creating a society where women can get back to work despite having little children, a society where there are necessary provisions to help them out. Finally, we'll have the cake and eat it too. Nothing will stop us from excelling in our work-life.

7

Transcendence: The Day My Fate Was Sealed

When it strikes, it strikes with vengeance. It peaks in the month of September. Nobody remains unaffected. It kills little children, and the world watches helplessly. There is nothing we can do about it. Or so we thought.

I remember coming across it twice. And on both occasions, we lost people who were extremely dear to us. We thought, like many other families in the region, that we were cursed. We were a large joint-family. We lived in the Gorakhpur district. We were agrarian and we barely made ends meet.

The first time I came across it was when it struck my six-year old nephew. I was in my early twenties then, and I already knew some friends and neighbours who had lost their children to Japanese Encephalitis. After having high fever for more than a day, my nephew suddenly fell unconscious. My father and I, who happened to be home at the time, rushed him to the medical college in the town. What I witnessed there was repulsive. The hospital was overcrowded, since it was the only tertiary-care centre for Japanese Encephalitis. Just like us, people kept rushing in carrying their relatives. Some were conscious, and would not stop vomiting. Some were declared dead upon arrival. My nephew was whisked away into the emergency room. But barely a few minutes later, we were informed that they could not save him.

The second time I came across it was when my grand-uncle complained of breathlessness and chest pain one day. When I brought him to the medical college in the town, the same scene greeted us. People rushed in with unconscious relatives, the corridors were full of people tending to their loved ones who were either unconscious or shivering uncontrollably. We were politely informed that several cases of Japanese Encephalitis were coming in by the hour, and that we were to find medical care elsewhere. On our way to another hospital, my grand-uncle died of a heart attack.

Although it isn't a nice way to look at things, the truth is that we could not have afforded to keep him alive had he survived. My grandmother's health was already taking a toll on the family's finances. Her weekly check-ups and her medicines burnt a huge hole in our pockets. We had to take a loan to stay afloat. We lived in fear because we knew very well that we were always one draught away from total ruin. Things were not under our control. It's a terrible experience to live with such a burden on your head, and it is something I wish nobody has to go through.

But you won't believe the number of people who have actually gone through it. The scarcity of good healthcare has made it so inaccessible that for several years, healthcare costs were steadily on the rise. And these rising healthcare costs made thirty nine million Indians poorer every year. In most cases, what set people back were aggressive interventions made at the end of people's lives. Scarcity and neglect for years together led to quick escalation, and people were not left with too many options. Most people had not even enrolled in an insurance scheme that they could fall back upon.

Private hospitals were not something most people could afford. But when it was a situation of life and death, that was the preferred option. There was a sense that the healthcare provided by the government lacked accountability. It wasn't completely unfounded. Without doubt, private healthcare has been more professional in India. To begin with, it has been less chaotic. It has been generally better maintained and much cleaner than government provided healthcare. But one must cut the government some slack. After all, they were the ones who kept their doors open for everyone. The more the people, the more the chaos. If they could be faulted for anything, it was that they weren't spreading themselves thin enough. Take the example of Gorakhpur itself, where the medical college in town was the go-to place for Japanese Encephalitis, not just for Gorakhpur but for several districts in Eastern Uttar Pradesh. To spread themselves thin, they required infrastructure. They required expertise. And they required that private healthcare became more accessible.

It wasn't just the costs of private healthcare which were staggering. The pharmaceutical industry was well-aware of just how much people depended on it. They, quite literally, made you pay for your life. Knowing that people would pay any price for their well-being, they fleeced us. I wish they had come home once and seen how we lived, and the sacrifices we made. Perhaps it would have prompted them to display some empathy.

As I enter my thirties now, Septembers aren't as bad as they used to be. Unlike in the past, when we dreaded the month of September because some acquaintance or the other would always lose their children to Japanese Encephalitis, we hear much less about it now. As children, we knew that if we wanted to live for long, we had to survive our first ten Septembers. Imagine what we have undergone, living our lives with that dreaded reality hanging over our heads. But the fight has been taken right into the enemy's territory, the enemy being Japanese Encephalitis. And slowly but surely, we are winning this battle.

In the past, when the annual outbreak used to make national headlines, several vaccination drives were launched. These drives must have saved the lives of many children, but these were temporary measures which didn't eradicate the disease completely. But of late, a comprehensive approach which goes to the roots of the issue has been adopted. I have been witness to it first hand, because this time, it isn't only a government initiative. They have realized that for a successful eradication, a lot rests with people on the ground.

To begin with, a large immunization drive was carried out. This wasn't like the ones before. The team did not simply go door to door, but checked and cross-checked with us several times. They were on a mission to immunize every child in the state. They were successful. This was followed by another team which came to our village. They went from house to house, sitting us down and giving us useful tips to prevent the disease. Much like some other diseases, pure drinking water and general cleanliness was key to avoiding Japanese Encephalitis. We were even shown some videos about it. Under the same programme, paramedics in the region were imparted special training, to ensure that they were adequately equipped to deal with the disease.

The entire programme was a huge shot in the arm for people who lived in Eastern Uttar Pradesh. But what you have to realize is that this did not cure us from all our ailments. In fact, all it did was to bring us at par with most other people in the country, who still suffered due to the lack of good healthcare. But what is bound to help our region in the long run is the All India Institute of Medical Sciences (AIIMS) which is coming up in Gorakhpur. As I told you before, when Japanese Encephalitis struck, the medical college in the town was not just Gorakhpur's only recourse but that of the entire region. This was a region which badly needed more healthcare infrastructure, and the AIIMS will bridge that gap in the long run. Twelve new AIIMS are coming up in different parts of the country, which means this gap will be bridged in several regions.

But the big change that is already benefiting us positively is the huge reduction in costs. The extent to which my grandmother's medicines used to set us back each month, has reduced considerably. The Jan Aushadhi Stores which have mushroomed across the country are a huge boon to families like us. Instead of going to fancy pharmacies and spending a substantial amount, most of us prefer the Jan Aushadhi Store these days. The government has set up these stores to provide generic drugs, which are equivalent in quality and efficacy, but which cost a fraction of what their branded counterparts used to cost. We end up saving thousands of rupees every month.

After all, it is a question of physical well-being, and of life and death. I am glad that the government has stepped in and is preventing families like ours, who belong to the aspiring class, to be fleeced. But more importantly, after many years, my grandmother's radiant smile has returned to her face. For years together, knowing how financially burdened we were and how her upkeep was costing us a bomb, she had considered herself to be a burden on the family. Our reassurances that we would pull through, that we were doing just fine, was not consolation enough. It is difficult to imagine what she was going through psychologically. She tried to stay out of the way, and just could not look us in the eyes. She was ashamed of herself, and the sad part of it was that it was no fault of hers. Things were beyond her control. She felt much better now. After years, she was returning to being her true self, the loving grandma we had known through our childhood.

We had a similar experience with my uncle, whose knees had taken a toll after years of hard-work on the farm. He got his first knee replacement surgery when I was a toddler, and it had cost the family a fortune. Thereafter he quietly bore the pain in his other knee for decades, knowing perfectly well that with the state of our finances and with the condition of my grandmother's health, it would be impossible for us to afford another knee replacement. One day, he just could not walk anymore. Since a bad knee was not life-threatening, we had to take a pragmatic decision. Was it more economical for us to forego an important component in the farm's workforce, or was it more economical to spend an astronomical amount but have him return to the workforce?

We discovered then that our math was not accurate, because the government had slashed the price of knee implants by seventy percent just months before. This would be a one-time payment, and that too of an amount which wasn't as big as what we had anticipated earlier. We went ahead with it, and our gamble paid off financially. It was a morale booster for the family as well. We were delighted to see my uncle hail and hearty again, back on his feet. The government had capped the price on knee implants, specialised cancer implants and heart stents. Millions of people were benefitting from the capped prices every year, and many like my uncle who could not have afforded it otherwise, found it to be within their reach. I was happy for people like us, who had been deprived of these basic solutions for years. Finally, someone was putting an end to unethical profiteering.

What I was most impressed about though, was the way things were taken care of when the neighbour's wife broke her foot. Just like us, our neighbours too had farmed the same piece of land for several generations, and we considered them to be part of the extended family. The neighbour's wife, whom we called 'chachi', had gone to the town one morning. On her way back, as she was getting off the bus, a two-wheeler ran over her foot. Chachi was in pain, but when we went to see her, she was more worried about the costs that they would incur. The family wanted to take her to the hospital, but she kept insisting that it was nothing. They finally took her to the hospital, and it turned out to be for the better, since she required urgent surgery without which she would have been unable to walk.

Just a year before the accident, when people from the local bank were going door to door and opening our bank accounts for the first time, they had offered two kinds of insurance along with the account. We didn't really bother back them, but our neighbours got themselves enrolled. The accidental insurance was priced at just twelve rupees per year. Luckily for chachi, she managed to get the surgery done for almost nothing at all, since the insurance took care of most of the cost.

When I heard about this, I took the entire family to the bank and got us enrolled for both the insurances. The second one was a life insurance, which cost three hundred and thirty rupees annually. Not only would things be taken care of if any one of us were to get into an accident, but if god forbid one of us were to lose our life, the family would receive two lakh rupees. This would substantially reduce any financial burden the family would face during the loss of a loved one. Especially if there was a costly medical intervention towards the end of anyone's life, the costs borne by the family would be taken care of.

When we returned from the bank that day, I felt extremely secure. In a short span of time, a family which was suffering and barely coping with the costs, was better off and quite secure financially. Right from childhood when Japanese Encephalitis could strike, to adolescence and adulthood where hard-work could weaken our hearts or literally bring us to our knees, to old age where one was accident prone, to even death, we were much more secure on all fronts than we had ever been. I felt empowered. I felt ready to give it my all, and to live without fear for the first time.

But all of this was the tip of the iceberg. Something much bigger and better was still to come. Honestly, having lived most of my life as someone who considered healthcare to be a huge burden on the family, someone who would never dare to step inside a private hospital, what was to come would be the biggest game changer of our times. It was nothing short of revolutionary.

Since the end of September 2018, my family and I are eligible for a benefit cover of five lakh rupees every year for secondary and tertiary care hospitalisation. The government under the Ayushman Bharat Yojana has created a network of hospitals, including private hospitals, which we could visit or get admitted to if we require medical care. Under the scheme, several pre and post hospitalisation expenses will also be taken care of. Considering that in most years we have spent much less than five lakh rupees on healthcare, it is safe to assume that henceforth we will avail quality healthcare completely free of cost.

Our family has been given a letter with a QR Code. Every hospital that has signed up for this scheme will have a special desk for us. There, we will have to present our letter, which they will scan. Instantly, they will know of our authenticity and eligibility. And thereafter, we will have access to the services we need for free. We will be able to avail of this scheme in any hospital that is part of Ayushman Bharat across the country. Even if we were traveling, and god forbid something were to happen, we would simply have to walk in to the nearest hospital that has enrolled in the scheme and present our QR code.

The scheme is completely cashless and paperless. To ensure that nobody is left out, there is no cap in the size of the family, or the age of the beneficiaries. It is believed that more than hundred million families from across the country will be entitled to this scheme. This translates into a whopping five hundred million of us being eligible. Who would have thought that forty percent of Indians, especially those who have trouble accessing good healthcare for various reasons, would be taken care of free of cost?

As part of this scheme, one and half lack wellness centres will be set up across the country. These centres would provide primary care to patients.

The government wants to have these centres in the remotest parts of the country, especially in certain areas which are quite far away from hospitals. These centres will have facilities like telemedicine, which will allow patients to get advice from specialists without having to travel too far. As of now, the scheme is slowly shaping up on the ground. But once it is up and running, people like me who could not dream of quality healthcare for most of our lives will have access to it free of cost.

Just a decade back, we used to live in fear. One never knew when Japanese Encephalitis would take one of our children away from us. One never knew how we would deal with people falling sick, getting injured or having accidents. We were at the mercy of the universe; we were slaves of our unfortunate circumstances. Things were not in our hands, and things could only get worse for us. We had resigned to our helpless fate.

When I look back, I can only hope that nobody has to ever go through this again. We are just as human as anyone else. Our financial condition can deprive us of several things, but there should be no compromise on healthcare. It isn't about the money or the politics, it is just the least we can do for each other as fellow humans. I'm glad that gradually, my country is taking this approach.

8

Decriminalizing Adultery: A Wife Is No Longer Her Husband's 'Property'

My name is Celina and I live in Hyderabad. I was one of the first crusaders against the 158-year-old draconian adultery law under Section 497 of the IPC that deemed adultery as a punishable offence committed by one man against another. Finally, the law that certified women to be treated as possessions rather than human beings has been abolished by India's Apex court in a historic judgement. I was an advocate against the law not because I was in a situation that involved adultery, but because the law violated basic rights of individuals, affecting dignity, privacy and equality of men and women thereby inviting the wrath of our constitution. All these years, according to law, men were the master of the wife and I found that manifestly arbitrary. The law gave power to a husband to control the sexuality of his lawfully wedded wife in order to assert this sole claim on her body. Monoandry, more than the protection of the sanctity of a social institution, therefore, seemed to be the basic premise of the law. Legal sovereignty of one sex over other another sex is absolutely wrong! Tradition cannot justify history.

On the other hand, Section 497 put the burden of guilt on the man who was in an adulterous relationship. The woman in question was considered innocent! Now, as all this drama ensues, I am not being a staunch feminist and standing by the women alone. In the pre adultery law decriminalizing era, men felt that it was unjust and that both parties – the man and the woman – should be held equally liable for the act. They did have a point. By assuming that the adulterous woman is blameless, it infantilized her, as though she were a helpless plaything in the hands of her home-wrecking lover. Also, according to the law, while a man can bring charges against his wife's paramour, the law did not grant the same privilege to the wronged wife. This was a brilliant, curveball piece of sexism, which happened to be unfair to men as well. Why was adultery criminalized in the first place when the act was between two consenting adults?

Besides the obvious gender discrimination, the law was problematic for several other reasons. A married man had the right to blame an outside agency for the breakdown of his marriage. If a wife has chosen to sleep outside her marriage, isn't it right that the couple looks at the inadequacies in their own relationship and not hold an outsider responsible for the breakdown of their marriage? And if the relationship has lost its foundation of trust, doesn't it make more sense that the couple approaches the courts for a mutual divorce than put a third person behind bars for breaking their marriage? The provided a psychological outlet to a spouse to blame a third person responsible for the failure of a marriage.

The definition of the adultery legislation in India, instituted by the British in the 1860s was so ambiguous that not only did people not know it existed in the first place, but when the judgement was passed and the act was decriminalized, people were lost in interpretation. The adultery law in India made me laugh. Adultery was treated differently, was a criminal offence, depending on your gender. Much of the Indian approach to criminalizing adultery comes from the colonial leftovers of British rule in India. It panders to the idea that women remain the property of their husbands, due to which their complicity in any adulterous act is immaterial. The only wrongdoers here are the men who bed women outside the confines of a marriage.

In 1954 the Supreme Court had refused to invalidate the adultery provisions because the petitioner was not an Indian citizen and targeting only husband was not violative of equality because special provisions could be made for women and children. Back in 1860 when the IPC was framed, a woman's position in society was extremely dismal. Accordingly, these laws are reflective of women's subservient social position that existed back then.

The entire penal code treats the female as the man's subordinate, a person with neither an independent identity nor an agency over her own body. The IPC specifically, was framed over a 150 years ago and reflects how men perceived women's social position at that time. Men believed a woman to be naïve and her will prone to manipulation. That's precisely why Section 497 was based on the premise that she can be tricked into indulging in adultery.

Patrilocality, where women move into their husband's homes makes them physically and emotionally vulnerable. On the other hand, men facing prolonged psychological, emotional and financial abuse by women is also a reality. My case here is not to abolish the institution of marriage. Most women and men get married by their own consent and wish, and most remain married throughout their lives. Moreover, for a person who believes in the divine nature of marriage, the right of marriage comes from the Constitution itself, where all are allowed to practice their faith without any prejudice. Just a few days ago I was reading the thriller novel Gone Girl by writer Gillian Flynn and I was thinking adultery is a great subject for books and movies. It bristles with possibilities – of love, lust, jealousy, fear, rage and so on. And it has huge potential for drama. In India, Section 497 of the Indian Penal Code, the law that dealt with adultery was astonishingly absurd. Here was a legal structure that most civilized countries dispensed with years ago. The law violated article 14 of our constitution since it created an irrational classification between men and women. In the present world, where women hold positions of authority in almost all spheres, the premise that the woman is always the victim not only undermined the notion of women's agency but also is entirely unfair to men.

There was an ancient notion that man was always the perpetrator and woman was always a victim of adultery. As luck would have it, the primeval opinion that had chauvinistic undertones and treated women as chattel holds no good today. As a woman myself, I strongly opinionated that Section 497 was destructive to woman's dignity, it denuded the woman to make choices. In the name of law, the law in adultery was merely a codified rule of patriarchy. It did not allow women to file a complaint against an adulterous husband who could otherwise misuse the law during matrimonial disputes such as divorce or civil cases relating to wives receiving maintenance.

History has been witness how men have blatantly filed criminal complaints against suspected or imagined men who they have alleged were having affairs with their wives. Whilst these charges could never be proved, it however ended up smearing the reputations of their estranged or divorced partners. Interestingly, Indian folklore and epics are full of stories about extra-marital love. Most love poems in Sanskrit are about illicit love. But Manusmriti, our ancient Hindu text, says: "If men persist in seeking intimate contact with other men's wives, the king should brand them with punishments that inspire terror and banish them". The law has been staggeringly sexist and crudely anti-women! Why should the legal system of a nation regulate whom one sleeps with?

India is still a very conservative country and without a doubt there have been quite a few people, people in my family, people I call friends who have backed the existence of adultery law and have argued that criminalization of adultery is important because it safeguards the institution of marriage. Here's my counter argument – section 497 only perpetrated the subordinate nature of women in a marriage. It is not whether the expectations of fidelity in a marriage are right or wrong or whether adultery denotes sexual freedom. It simply is whether the state can and should monitor a relationship between adults that is too complex, sensitive and individual for it to be capable of doing in a just manner. What if a married man has consensual sex with another woman who is unmarried? I believe the only time the State should be in your bedroom is in a situation when consent is amiss.

When will we stop hearing sermons about the sanctity of marriage and their implied homilies that we need to put up with all sorts of injustices for its sake? The same old campaigning is cited each time there is a demand for a law against marital rape. You can't criminalize a man who rapes his wife, so goes the argument, simply because marriage is a sacrament. The entire point is that law should punish violence and coercion – not acts of free will between two consenting adults. And, adultery is undoubtedly a consensual act. What about live-in relationships that are legal in India? Though the common man is still hesitant in accepting this kind of relationship, the Protection of Women from Domestic Violence Act provides for the protection and maintenance thereby granting the right of alimony to an aggrieved live-in partner.

When this deliberation over whether to or not to decriminalize the adultery law was in progress, I remember reading in the paper one day how whilst hearing the argument, the Chief Justice remarked that scraping the law in its entirety may affect the sanctity of the marriage. It is remarkable to hear esteemed justices talk about the sanctity of marriage, when the court itself that has had to push in reforms to protect married women from the abuse they have suffered as a part of getting into this sanctified contract!

From domestic violence legislation debates to dowry debates in Parliament, our leaders have had to fight not only for the protection of spouses in an environment that's almost perfected for prolonged psychological, physical and emotional abuse, but also the semi-religious idea of the divine nature of marriage. It is to fix the abuses and suffering endured under this divine contract that extensive laws have had to be made that include Domestic Violence Act 2005, Dowry Prohibition Act, 1961 and Prohibition of Child Marriage Act, 1961.

The treatment of adultery under Indian penal law has risen from an archaic sense of preservation of a woman's sexuality in order to refrain from tempting a man's lust. Women, and by extension their sexuality, remained the property of their husbands alone. All said and done, why do we forget that emotional cheating is far more devastating than physical cheating? Most people, especially women thrive on the emotional connection they build with their partner. That forms the foundation of their relationship, not the sexual connection they share.

At a time when movements like Time's Up and MeToo against sexual harassment and assault are taking place in full force, law such as this were a horrendous example of gender discrimination. What baffles me more is, how did this law continue to survive in our statute books for so long, at a time when people are tirelessly trumpeting their support for women's empowerment and women are finally fulfilling their tryst with destiny? From privacy to adultery, triple talaq to Sabarimala, the Supreme Court of India has been proactive in protecting and promoting women's rights. About time!

Like marriage, adultery is undergoing a change of image. The number of countries considering adultery to be a criminal offense is steadily coming down, Government benefits given to married couples are being reconsidered, divorce is becoming more acceptable, religious beliefs and their impact on morality are being continuously challenged and there is an increased access to people than ever before.

Criminalising consensual sexual relations was not the only provision that made the law archaic: It allowed only a man to prosecute another man for the act of committing adultery with his wife. Punishment could range up to 5 years of imprisonment, fine or both. Men's rights groups had time and again hailed the decision of the Supreme Court to reconsider the law, since they believed the provision of only men getting jailed is discriminatory and violated Article 14 of the Constitution. It was blatantly not just anti-women, but also prejudiced the notion of autonomy that a married woman had over her own body. This is precisely what today lies at the heart of the marital rape debate in India and the abortion deliberations across the world. The idea that adultery as an offence should be gender neutral where both men and women should be held responsible for the independent choices they make for themselves is perfectly reasonable.

We have to understand the fact that law is not absolute in nature, it is progressive. In India, the Supreme Court, one of the most vital institutions, the tip of a very large pyramid of local and appellate courts has nudged the country ahead in a progressive direction with its recent rulings. In a vast and chaotic democracy of 1.3 billion people, in just the space of a few months, the apex court has sought to wipe out generations of prejudice. It decriminalized gay sex, told a Hindu temple it couldn't bar entry to women of menstruating age and overturned a 158-year-old adultery law that treated wives as their husbands' property. In a complex and chaotic country, India's highest court has long battled charges of being too beholden to politicians in power and willing to trample on civil liberties when the government demands it. With its recent rulings, the court has reasserted itself as a protector of the individual rights promised by India's 70-year-old constitution.

In India, women who comprise 49% of the electorate are being felicitated and celebrated. Remember how Budget 2018-19 was all about women? Our government at the helm has had a powerful track record on empowering women through highly effective schemes like Beti Bachao Beti Padao, Ujjwala Yojana, Stand Up India and Swachh Bharat. From Mann Ki Baat to Independence Day speeches, our leader has always been vocal about the achievements that women have triumphed – in Parliament, sports, judiciary, army, and grassroots – and how they are transforming India and building India 2.0.

Today, women are breaking glass ceilings and working tirelessly to catapult themselves forward in every sphere. They must be supported by a strong statutory backing. A gender-neutral legal framework can play a pivotal role in gradually transforming regressive social and moral norms about women. It is high time we take steps to protect the sexual rights of women. One significant step would be to recognize them. The fact that either partner in a relationship, that is, the husband or the wife may choose to indulge in adultery, b. to recognize that adultery is a consensual act between two persons and c. to recognize that it is not a criminal act but rather a breach of trust between the husband and the wife, where the only remedy for the aggrieved should be filing for a divorce. The steps being taken today are merely an attempt to correct the power equation, the everyday imbalances thus far that has triggered it, altering history which has been witness to unexpressed and unacknowledged feelings. Gender equations have for long determined the value systems that govern our societal structures. It is a profound shift in the narrative, and I have a strong belief, its impact will be felt sharply.

www.ingramcontent.com/pod-product-compliance
Lightning Source LLC
Chambersburg PA
CBHW031321250726
48656CB00005B/1913